Faithbuilders Bible Studies

The Gospel of Mark

by Mathew Bartlett & Derek Williams

Copyright © 2015 Mathew Bartlett & Derek Williams.

FAITHBUILDERS PUBLISHING
12 Dukes Court, Bognor Road
Chichester, PO19 8FX, United Kingdom
www.faithbuilderspublishing.co.uk

ISBN: 978-1-910942-08-6

A catalogue record for this book is available from the British Library

Cover Design by Blitz Media, Pontypool, Torfaen, UK

Printed and bound in Great Britain

Dedicated to all those who are hungry for God's Word.

More from Faithbuilders Bible Studies

Faithbuilders Bible studies: Mark

Esther – Queen of Persia

The Prophecy of Amos – A Warning for Today

Zechariah – Prophet of Messiah

Faithbuilders Bible Studies

The Faithbuilders Bible study series has been developed a useful resource for today's students of God's Word and their busy lifestyles. Pastors, home or study group leaders and indeed for anyone wishing to study the Bible for themselves will benefit from using Faithbuilders studies.

Each volume is the result of many years of group Bible study, and has been revised again and again to be relevant, challenging and faith building whilst remaining clear and easy to understand, helping more people to discover the blessings of God's Word.

Mathew Bartlett holds a Master's Degree in Biblical Studies from the University of Chester, England. Derek Williams is now retired, having been a pastor and preacher for over 40 years.

Contents

Mark Chapter 1

Introduction

1:1 The beginning of the gospel of Jesus Christ, the Son of God.

Here we have the title of the book; it is not actually the gospel of Mark but the gospel (good news) about Jesus Christ. Mark declares that the promises God had made throughout the Old Testament of a coming deliverer (e.g. Gen. 3:15) had been fulfilled by the coming of Jesus Christ. So the good news is all about Jesus.

In Hebrew, the name "Jesus" is "Jeshua" which means "Jehovah is salvation". This is the name that the angel told Joseph to give to the child born of the Virgin Mary; "for he shall save his people from their sins" (Matt. 1:21).

Mark calls Jesus the "Christ", the one anointed by God to become the saviour of world through his death and resurrection. In the beginning of Mark's gospel we also see that Jesus is called the "Son of God". The apostle Paul also preached that Jesus was the Son of God (e.g. Acts 9:20). Such is the importance of this Christian belief that 1 John 4:15 tells us "whoever confesses that Jesus is the Son of God, God dwells in him and he dwells in God." It is as Son of God that Jesus embodies the perfect image of his Father (Heb. 1:3).

Old Testament Prophecy Fulfilled

1:2–3 As it is written in Isaiah the prophet, 'Look, I am sending my messenger ahead of you, who will prepare your way, the voice of one shouting in the wilderness, 'Prepare the way for the Lord, make his paths straight.'

Mark unites the Old Testament with the new to show that the new is a fulfilment of the old (Matt. 5:17). The quotations from Malachi 3:1 and

Isaiah 40:3 refer to John the Baptist as the forerunner of Christ; the one who came before him as a herald to announce the arrival of the Saviour and to prepare the hearts of the people to receive him. In those days heralds were employed to run before reigning monarchs to clear a pathway for them so that they were not hindered in their journey. John was sent to remove the obstacles of sin and unbelief from the people of Israel so that they might be ready to accept the Christ. He did not take his message to the towns and cities to be heard, but into the wilderness. His message was that the people should return to God by turning from their sin. John was to make the way straight for Jesus by calling the people to a change of heart which would result in a change of conduct.

1:4–5 In the wilderness John the baptizer began preaching a baptism of repentance for the forgiveness of sins. People from the whole Judean countryside and all of Jerusalem were going out to him, and he was baptizing them in the Jordan River as they confessed their sins.

John told them that they needed to repent, that is, "a change of one's mind for the better and heartily to amend one's ways with abhorrence of past sins in order to obtain forgiveness of and release from sins" (Amp. N. T.). John's baptism was not Christian baptism as we know it today, but an outward sign that those who came to him had responded to his message with repentance. It is clear from Matthew 3:7–8 that John demanded the peoples' lives be changed to show that their repentance was genuine. Notice that John did not go to the people, but they came to him from every city, town and village throughout Judah (it would seem as if this was through the influence of the Holy Spirit); and on confession of their sins he baptised the repentant in the Jordan River.

John's Abode and Appearance

1:6 John wore a garment made of camel's hair with a leather belt around his waist, and he ate locusts and wild honey.

John's dwelling place, dress and food showed him to be a prophet after the order of Elijah (2 Kings 1:8) and he was recognised at once being a messenger from the Lord.

Pre-eminence of Christ

1:7 He proclaimed, 'One more powerful than I am is coming after me; I am not worthy to bend down and untie the strap of his sandals.

John made it very clear that he had not come to project his own image but that he was merely the signpost to the one that was coming after him, Jesus Christ. He was very conscious of his own unworthiness and esteemed himself of no value compared to the one that would come in power and who would far exceed him and anything that he could achieve.

1:8 I baptize you with water, but he will baptize you with the Holy Spirit.

Here we have the first mention of the promise of the baptism of the Holy Spirit. John baptised in water, but it is only Jesus Christ who can baptise with the Holy Spirit and fire (Acts 2:38). This verse can be taken as an assertion of Christ's divinity—for only God can be said to be the giver of the Spirit of God.

Christ's Baptism and Temptation

1:9 Now in those days Jesus came from Nazareth in Galilee and was baptized by John in the Jordan River.

Jesus came to John to be baptised; not for the remission of his sins, for he had none (2 Cor. 5:21; Heb. 4:15). He came rather because he had a desire to "fulfil all righteousness" (Matt. 3:15).

1:10–11 And just as Jesus was coming up out of the water, he saw the heavens splitting apart and the Spirit descending on him like a dove. And a voice came from heaven: 'You are my one dear Son; in you I take great delight.'

In this verse is depicted the Christian belief of God as a trinity: God the Son (Jesus) is seen coming up out of the water as God the Holy Spirit descends on him and God the Father speaks to him from heaven. The voice of God confirmed Jesus to be his only beloved Son with whom he was well pleased.

1:12–13 The Spirit immediately drove him into the wilderness. He was in the wilderness forty days, enduring temptations from Satan. He was with wild animals, and angels were ministering to his needs.

Immediately after the Holy Spirit came on Jesus, he (that is, the Spirit) impelled Christ to go into the wilderness, where he remained for forty days and nights being tempted by Satan. This "corresponds to the forty years of testing that Israel endured in the desert" (A. Cole). The desert to the Hebrew was a place of gloomy terror, the abode of devils and wild beasts; a place to be avoided. During all this time God protected his Son (Psalm 91:11); and after he had faced the temptations of Satan the angels of God came and ministered to him. Both Matthew 4 and Luke 4 provide further details of this temptation of Christ.

John the Baptist came before the first appearance of Christ to prepare the way for him by preaching repentance. Today, we can prepare others in a similar way for the second coming of Christ by living a life that reflects his character and by preaching the gospel message. Our hope is that others may come to know Jesus as their Saviour. John said "I must decrease but he must increase" (John 3:30) and to be good witnesses like John, we too must wear humility as a cloak, allowing the Lord to reign in every area of our lives. When this is so, it will be "no longer I who lives but Christ who lives in me" (Gal. 2:20); God will be able to use us in whatever way he will.

Whenever we are tempted and tried, let us remember that Jesus understands, for he suffered the same temptations that we do, so that he might help us in time of need (Heb. 2:18). God has sent his angels to watch over us and minister to us (Heb. 1:14).

Christ's Message

1:14 Now after John was imprisoned, Jesus went into Galilee and proclaimed the gospel of God.

God's ways are not our ways; his ways are past finding out. Therefore we cannot fully understand why it was that John was removed from the scene by being put in prison and eventually beheaded. Yet it was at this point in time that Jesus started his ministry. It was not to Judea, the most important region, nor to Jerusalem, but to Galilee that Jesus went. Galilee is seen by some commentators as a picture of spiritual bondage, as historically it had always been the first area to fall into the hands of invaders. It was this region of spiritual darkness that the prophet Isaiah foretold would first receive the light (Isaiah 9:1–2).

1:15 He said, 'The time is fulfilled and the kingdom of God is near. Repent and believe the gospel!'

Jesus's message differed from John's in as much as Jesus brought the "good news"; indeed, he was the good news! Christ had come to make a way for people to enter the kingdom of God so that through him we might be able to live the life of that kingdom. This kingdom would be found within the hearts of people (Luke 17:21); for it was not an earthly kingdom but a heavenly (or spiritual) one (John 18:36, Rom. 14:17). Jesus proclaimed that the hour had come which all the prophets had pointed to: the kingdom of God had come, for the king had arrived. Like John, Jesus called the people to repent so that they could have their sins forgiven. But Jesus added one thing more; he said, "Believe the gospel". They were to believe on him as the Son of God, the promised one; the way into God's kingdom (John 14:6).

The Call of the First Disciples

1:16 As he went along the Sea of Galilee, he saw Simon and Andrew, Simon's brother, casting a net into the sea (for they were fishermen).

It was not by chance that Jesus walked by the Sea of Galilee; he purposed to do so that he might call these men to follow him. Simon, Andrew, James and John were about their daily work, what they had been doing since they were old enough to go fishing and what they expected to be doing for the rest of their lives; but Jesus had other plans for them. So it can be with us. We may have been doing the same thing for ages never expecting anything different to happen, and then Jesus comes along and changes our lives.

1:17–20 Jesus said to them, 'Follow me, and I will turn you into fishers of people.' They left their nets immediately and followed him. Going on a little farther, he saw James, the son of Zebedee, and John his brother in their boat mending nets. Immediately he called them, and they left their father Zebedee in the boat with the hired men and followed him.

This was probably not the first time that these disciples had seen Jesus. They may have been present when he was baptised by John, but they certainly would not yet have known Jesus well. Nevertheless, at his bidding they immediately left what they were doing (their livelihood) and followed him. He would teach them the new trade of winning souls. "They abandoned all that they held dear, and all earthly security in simple committal to Christ" (A. Cole). This is the minimum requirement for every Christian (Luke 14:33).

A Demonic Delivered

1:21 Then they went to Capernaum. When the Sabbath came, Jesus went into the synagogue and began to teach.

It was the consistent practice of Jesus to attend the synagogue and the temple, and on this Sabbath, being in Capernaum, it was to the local synagogue he went. This may have been the same synagogue which Luke informs us had been built by a Roman centurion (whose servant was healed in Luke 7:2–10). It was customary in the meeting for the Rabbi to invite someone to read and explain the scriptures. So Jesus would have done this by invitation.

1:22 The people there were amazed by his teaching, because he taught them like one who had authority, not like the experts in the law.

This was no ordinary meeting and no ordinary teacher, for he spoke to them as one who not only knew the scriptures but also the full truth of them, which the scribes did not. The words came from him with life and power and the people were astounded; even the powers of darkness were stirred up.

1:23 Just then there was a man in their synagogue with an unclean spirit, and he cried out,

It would appear from this verse that the man was a regular attendee at the synagogue and would have been well known. It was the demon within the man that cried out (not the man) and made itself known to Jesus.

1:24 'Leave us alone, Jesus the Nazarene! Have you come to destroy us? I know who you are — the Holy One of God!'

The first thing he cried was for Jesus to "leave us alone". As there is only one demon mentioned in verse 23, 25 and 26 the "us" might possibly be a reference to the man and the demon (unless the demon is speaking on behalf of his kind). "What have we to do with you" that is, "what have we got in common with you?" Of course the answer is "nothing" for Jesus is pure—the demon unclean; Jesus is light—the demon darkness; Jesus came from God—the demon from the devil; and Jesus came from heaven—the demon from hell. The demon addressed Jesus in the first instance by his earthly name "Jesus of Nazareth". He knew that Christ had come to destroy all the works of the devil (1 John 3:8); and he confessed who Jesus was (James 2:19). Since all power has been given to Jesus in heaven and earth, even demons are compelled to obey him.

1:25 But Jesus rebuked him: 'Silence! Come out of him!'

Note that Jesus did not lay hands on the man—and he did not speak to him, only to the demon—nor did he pray for him. He rebuked the unclean spirit by commanding him to shut up, or "be muzzled", and then to come out of the man.

1:26 After throwing him into convulsions, the unclean spirit cried out with a loud voice and came out of him.

The demon could not do any other than obey Jesus' command. As he left the man, he convulsed him violently and gave a loud screech. The power of the Lord Jesus caused the demon to be wrenched away from the man.

1:27 They were all amazed so that they asked each other, 'What is this? A new teaching with authority! He even commands the unclean spirits and they obey him.'

The man was set free! This deliverance caused a great stir among the people, for although they had most probably seen the priests exorcising unclean spirits, this was the first time that they had witnessed someone actually having authority over them and casting them out by his word of command.

1:28 So the news about him spread quickly throughout all the region around Galilee.

This demonstration of the power and authority of Jesus caused his fame to spread right throughout Galilee. But although the people were amazed and wondered at these things, Mark does not say that they believed on him.

At Simon Peter's House

1:29–30 Now as soon as they left the synagogue, they entered Simon and Andrew's house, with James and John. Simon's mother-in-law was lying down, sick with a fever, so they spoke to Jesus at once about her.

These verses tell us a few details concerning Simon's home and family. From all that is recorded of Simon Peter we see that he was a rough and ready kind of person, often getting things wrong. Yet here we see him as a tender and caring family man. He not only provided a home for his widowed mother-in-law but also for his brother Andrew, so we can assume that the brothers' parents were dead (see 1 Tim. 5:8). He was also hospitable, for he invited Jesus, James and John back to his home for a meal (1 Pet. 4:9; Rom. 12:13).

However things we not well at home and the household were not prepared for visitors. Peter's mother-in-law had a fever and so was bed-ridden. Although they had known Jesus only for a short time they immediately brought this problem to him and had faith to believe that he would heal her.

1:31 He came and raised her up by gently taking her hand. Then the fever left her and she began to serve them.

Jesus did not pray or speak with her he just took hold of her hand and she was immediately healed. There are other recorded incidents when Jesus healed and raised people from the dead by taking them by the hand (e.g. Matt. 9:25). The mother-in-law wasted no time in recovering; she helped to wait on them, serving them food, as many other women would do throughout Christ's ministry.

1:32–33 When it was evening, after sunset, they brought to him all who were sick and demon-possessed. The whole town gathered by the door.

Following the miracle in the synagogue and the healings in the home, news of Christ's power spread quickly throughout Capernaum and by the evening everybody that was sick or demon possessed was brought to Jesus at Simon's home. He turned no one away but ministered to them all.

1:34 So he healed many who were sick with various diseases and drove out many demons. But he would not permit the demons to speak, because they knew him.

Yet it is not certain from the text that all were healed, for the verse says "many" and not "all". It is Matthew who insists (citing the same incident) that every sick person, without exception, was healed (Matt. 8:16). Once again Jesus would not allow the demons to bear witness to who he was for they did so by compulsion and not voluntarily. "Christ is prepared to await the revelation to be made by God to men that alone will enable them to say with Peter, 'you are the Christ' (Mark 8:29). Demons may well believe but they do not trust" (A. Cole).

Secret Prayer

1:35 Then Jesus got up early in the morning when it was still very dark, departed, and went out to a deserted place, and there he spent time in prayer.

After such an eventful day, during which much power had gone out from him (Mark 5:30), Jesus arose earlier than anyone else (before dawn) and went to a secluded place so that he could talk with his heavenly Father in peace without interruption. From various accounts in the gospels we know that he did this regularly (e.g. Luke 6:12). If our Lord found it necessary to have quiet times alone with God the Father, how much more should we seek to have such times?

He Came to Preach

1:36–39 Simon and his companions searched for him. When they found him, they said, 'Everyone is looking for you.' He replied, 'Let us go elsewhere, into the surrounding villages, so that I can preach there too. For that is what I came out here to do.'

On awaking and finding Jesus not there, Simon Peter and the others sought him out. They could not understand why he should take himself away when so many people were seeking him to be healed. Imagine the disciples' surprise when he told them that they must go away from the publicity in Capernaum and preach elsewhere. Christ's purpose in coming into the world was to preach the good news of the kingdom of God. His mission was to seek the lost and to save the souls of men, not only to heal (Isaiah 61:1; Luke 19:10; John 12:47).

So he departed from Capernaum and preached in all the synagogues throughout Galilee, continuing to deliver those possessed by demons.

A Leper Healed

1:40 Now a leper came to him and fell to his knees, asking for help. 'If you are willing, you can make me clean,' he said.

In this encounter it would seem to be only Jesus and the leper involved; which is understandable as no one would go near anybody suffering with this supposedly contagious and foul smelling disease. Lepers were completely isolated from society according to the law (Lev. 13:46). Indeed, by approaching Jesus this man was in violation of the law; but Jesus, who came to fulfil the law, did not rebuke him. As he came to Jesus in all humility and reverence, on his knees begging to be healed, he had no doubt about Jesus' ability to heal, only about his willingness.

1:41–42 Moved with compassion, Jesus stretched out his hand and touched him, saying, 'I am willing. Be clean!' The leprosy left him at once, and he was clean.

With a heart overflowing with compassion, Jesus did what no other would dare to do. He touched the man, and by doing so he put himself in peril, not so much of catching the disease as of being an outcast. A heart that is full of the compassion of Christ will dare to do anything in his name. The touch of the Saviour's hand and the comforting and longed for words "I am willing, be clean" made the man whole.

1:43–44 Immediately Jesus sent the man away with a very strong warning. He told him, 'See that you do not say anything to anyone, but go, show yourself to a priest, and bring the offering that Moses commanded for your cleansing, as a testimony to them.'

If we were healed in such a way the first thing we would want to do after giving thanks to God is let others know. But Jesus strictly ordered this man not to tell anyone about his cleansing from leprosy. Instead, in fulfilment of the law he was to show himself to the priest, who would thoroughly examine him to make certain that he was completely healed before making an offering for his cleansing (Lev. 14:2–32). This would be proof to the people that he really was healed.

1:45 But as the man went out he began to announce it publicly and spread the story widely, so that Jesus was no longer able to enter any town openly but stayed outside in remote places. Still they kept coming to him from everywhere.

This man did exactly opposite to what Jesus had ordered him, and because of this the news spread like a fire and Jesus could no longer go into a town because of the huge crowds. Instead he stayed outside in the desert places where the people kept coming to him from everywhere to be healed or delivered. Any disobedience to Christ, from whatever motive, will always have the effect of hindering rather than helping the cause of God's kingdom.

Discussion Questions for Chapter 1

1. vv. 1–45. List those who, in this section of Mark's gospel, give witness that Jesus Christ is the Son of God (don't forget 1:10–11).

2. vv. 10–11. How can you be sure that Jesus Christ was without sin?

3. vv. 1–45. In what ways does Mark (in chapter 1) show Jesus as someone greater than John?

4. vv. 36–39. Why do you think Jesus chose to leave behind, rather than stay and build on, the apparent success of his ministry in Capernaum?

5. vv. 1–45. In what ways does Christ demonstrate His authority in the first chapter of Mark?

You will find suggested answers to the study questions on pages 183–193.

Mark Chapter 2

Paralytic Healed

2:1–2 Now after some days, when he returned to Capernaum, the news spread that he was at home. So many gathered that there was no longer any room, not even by the door, and he preached the word to them.

After all the excitement in Capernaum had calmed down, Jesus returned there; most probably he stayed again at Peter's house. As soon as it became known that he was there multitudes of people came to him, filling and surrounding the house. This time the people came not just to be healed but to be taught and receive the word of God. Most of these people had been healed already! Nevertheless wherever and whenever there was a need of healing Jesus responded, for healing was one of the signs to say that he was the Messiah (Luke 7:22).

2:3–4 Some people came bringing to him a paralytic, carried by four of them. When they were not able to bring him in because of the crowd, they removed the roof above Jesus. Then, after tearing it out, they lowered the stretcher the paralytic was lying on.

As Jesus was preaching, four men arrived carrying a friend who was completely paralysed. It would seem that he was unable to do anything for himself and so most probably had be fed, clothed and washed by his friends; he could not move any part of his body. The man's comrades had heard about Jesus' healing power and came expecting their friend to be healed. When they arrived at Simon's house, Jesus was in the middle of preaching, and there was no way they could get through the crowd. But their faith was so great that they were determined to bring him to Jesus by any means. There are instances like this that obstinacy and stubbornness can be good traits; but only if they are directed towards doing right and acting in faith toward God. These men did not give up but persevered until they accomplished what they set out to do—even if it meant carrying their friend up to the roof, tearing it apart and lowering him down on ropes to the feet of Jesus. Like them, we must never give up our acts of faith and service to God (Gal. 6:9).

2:5 When Jesus saw their faith, he said to the paralytic, 'Son, your sins are forgiven.'

Seeing the faith of the man and his friends, Jesus responded. He saw beyond the physical need of the man, and we might suppose that the man himself was more conscious of his spiritual need that his physical. Perhaps this is why the Lord does not say "be healed" as the people expected him to but "your sins are forgiven you".

2:6–7 Now some of the experts in the law were sitting there, turning these things over in their minds: 'Why does this man speak this way? He is blaspheming! Who can forgive sins but God alone?'

This caused a stir among some of the teachers in the crowd (though not all of them). They began to reason in their minds the implications of what Jesus had just said. According to their knowledge of the scriptures no one could forgive sins (remove guilt, remit the penalty of sin and bestow righteousness) except God; by making this statement Jesus was claiming the prerogative of God and so in their minds was guilty of blasphemy.

Yet since Jesus Christ is God manifest in the flesh (1 Tim. 3:16) the prerogative to forgive sins is always his. Moreover, because he is the Son of God he knew that his mission in coming into the world would be achieved and that nothing would stop him obtaining salvation for us. Perhaps it was on the strength of this foreknowledge that Jesus could say, even before the cross, "your sins are forgiven you".

2:8 Now immediately, when Jesus realized in his spirit that they were contemplating such thoughts, he said to them, 'Why are you thinking such things in your hearts

Although they did not openly speak, Jesus knew what the teachers of the law were thinking in their hearts and minds (John 2:25); so he questioned their reasoning.

2:9 Which is easier, to say to the paralytic, 'Your sins are forgiven,' or to say, 'Stand up, take your stretcher, and walk'?

Since they incessantly demanded signs from Jesus, demanding infallible proof that he was who he claimed to be (Mark 8:11), Jesus decided to give them a sign they had not asked for. When he asked them which was easier to say "your sins are forgiven" or "be healed", they did not answer him. Evidently, it is equally easy to say both, and divine power could justify either statement. Nevertheless, there is no outward sign by which the reality of forgiveness of sins can be tested; whilst it is obvious to all whether a man can walk or not. So although forgiveness was more important, only by healing the man's body could Jesus prove the validity of his claims. Cole remarks, "A prophet might heal, but no mere prophet could ever forgive sins."

2:10–12 But so that you may know that the Son of Man has authority on earth to forgive sins,' — he said to the paralytic — I tell you, stand up, take your stretcher, and go home.' And immediately the man stood up, took his stretcher, and went out in front of them all. They were all amazed and glorified God, saying, 'We have never seen anything like this!

In order to demonstrate his authority as the Son of God; having the right to forgive sins, Jesus turned to the man and told him to arise, pick up his bed and go home. He immediately did so, much to the amazement of the people, who gave glory to God.

2:13 Jesus went out again by the sea. The whole crowd came to him, and he taught them.

Jesus next went to the seaside and was followed by the crowds, to whom he taught the things of God. In Mark 1:4 we saw that Jesus "*heralded*" the good news (as in Mark 1:21). He *teaches* in Mark 2:2 and in this verse he *speaks* the word. From the use of these three different terms we can say that Jesus evangelised, instructed from the scriptures and he informally taught the people.

Another Disciple Chosen

2:14 As he went along, he saw Levi, the son of Alphaeus, sitting at the tax booth. 'Follow me,' he said to him. And he got up and followed him.

As with the other disciples Jesus did not just pass by or happen to see Levi (also called Matthew); he had planned this meeting. The other disciples were fishermen, but Levi was an entirely a different kettle of fish! He was one of the despised tax collectors, a man who collected wealth for the Romans. Many people would have been shocked to see Jesus calling him. Tax collectors were usually greedy and immoral. Nevertheless, when he was called, Levi immediately left his job and followed Jesus.

2:15 As Jesus was having a meal in Levi's home, many tax collectors and sinners were eating with Jesus and his disciples, for there were many who followed him.

From Luke 5:29 it seems that this feast was put on by Levi so that his old business acquaintances might have an opportunity to meet Jesus; and indeed he seems to have introduced a great many to his new master.

2:16 When the experts in the law and the Pharisees saw that he was eating with sinners and tax collectors, they said to his disciples, 'Why does he eat with tax collectors and sinners?'

This incited the wrath and criticism of the Pharisees; in their eyes Jesus was contaminating himself by mixing with notorious sinners and tax collectors. We know from the story of the Good Samaritan that neither the priest nor Levite would help the man attacked by robbers in case they became ceremonially unclean (Luke 10:30–37). But the Pharisees were wrong in their judgment of Christ for firstly, whenever a person became a friend or follower of the Lord Jesus they turned from their sins; and secondly, Jesus needed to be among this kind of people, for their need of him was great.

2:17 When Jesus heard this he said to them, 'Those who are healthy don't need a physician, but those who are sick do. I have not come to call the righteous, but sinners.'

When Jesus became aware of their criticism, he told them that it was for the sake of the lost and for sinners that he had come into the world (Luke 19:10); to call them to repent and be saved. It is such people who are most conscious of their need of salvation, whereas the self-righteous have no sense of their need. Only a sick person needs a doctor; those who are healthy do not. Jesus was not suggesting that the religious leaders did not need God's forgiveness, but rather that they needed to have their eyes and hearts opened to the truth about their own condition before God—"for all have sinned and come short of the glory of God" (Rom. 3:23).

2:18 Now John's disciples and the Pharisees were fasting. So they came to Jesus and said, 'Why do the disciples of John and the disciples of the Pharisees fast, but your disciples don't fast?'

John the Baptist, together with his disciples (like the Pharisees) rigidly kept to the ceremonial laws of the Jewish religion. Several of the Lord's disciples had previously been followers of John, and although it was not required by the law that a man should fast every week, it had become an important practice of many devoted Jews. Here we see some of John's disciples joining the Pharisees by questioning Jesus about why his followers did not observe this custom of fasting.

The First New Thing

2:19 Jesus said to them, 'The wedding guests cannot fast while the bridegroom is with them, can they? As long as they have the bridegroom with them they do not fast.

In reply Jesus used this illustration; that of a bridegroom at a wedding. "How can the friends fast while they are rejoicing in the presence of the bridegroom?" he asks. Here Jesus refers to himself as the bridegroom (as he also does in the parable of the ten virgins in Matthew 25:1–6), and the church is his bride (2 Cor. 11:2; Rev. 21:2; Rev. 22:17). As long as Jesus was with the disciples they could not fast; for weddings are meant to be joyful occasions whilst fasting is a sign either of some terrible disaster or of voluntary abasement. As Cole observes, "in a time of joyous fellowship who thinks of fasting?" In Hebrew weddings the friends remained with the bridegroom throughout the celebration feast, which could last from seven to fourteen days, before taking away his bride to the bridal chamber to consummate the marriage.

2:20 But the days are coming when the bridegroom will be taken from them, and at that time they will fast.

Yet Jesus foretells that the day would come when he would be taken away from his disciples and be crucified; then would be the time for them to mourn and fast (John 16:20). There is a right time for everything (Eccl. 3:1–4).

Second New Thing

2:21 No one sews a patch of unshrunk cloth on an old garment; otherwise, the patch pulls away from it, the new from the old, and the tear becomes worse.

For the first time in his ministry, Jesus clearly speaks of introducing a new covenant which would entirely replace the old. Although this had been foretold in the Old Testament (Jer. 31:31) the religious leaders of his day were still not prepared to accept it.

Jesus describes the nature of this new covenant by comparing it to a new piece of cloth. Just as no one sews a new piece of cloth onto an old garment so the new covenant would not be a patched up version of the old. Nor would it be a sect within the Jewish religion. The result of an attempt to modify the old covenant would be to make matters worse. The problem of the spiritual state of humankind would not be addressed, and the gap between Jew and Gentile would remain or become even greater. Instead, part of the plan of the new covenant was for Christ to "reconcile to God both [Jew and Gentile, united] in a single body by means of his cross; thereby killing the mutual enmity and bringing the feud to an end" (Eph. 2:14–16). Only a completely new covenant could do away with the old (Heb. 8:13), so that God's law could be written in the hearts of every person (Heb. 8:10, 10:16).

Third New Thing

2:22 And no one pours new wine into old wineskins; otherwise, the wine will burst the skins, and both the wine and the skins will be destroyed. Instead new wine is poured into new wineskins.'

Here Jesus uses another illustration to show the blessings of the new covenant. In this one, he speaks of putting new wine into new bottles. The new wine which Jesus brings to us is the Holy Spirit (Luke 3:16). In Acts 2:13 those who received the Holy Spirit on the day of Pentecost were thought to be drunk with new wine. Only those who are born again of the Spirit of God, who are new creatures in Christ Jesus (2 Cor. 5:17; Gal. 6:15) can be filled with the Holy Spirit and are able to contain him without being destroyed by the holiness of God.

The Sabbath Day

2:23 Jesus was going through the grain fields on a Sabbath, and his disciples began to pick some heads of wheat as they made their way.

On a certain day, the disciples were feeling hungry, and so as they passed through corn fields, they plucked the ears of corn, rubbed off the husks in their hands and ate the grain, as was permitted by the law of Moses (Deut. 23:25).

2:24 So the Pharisees said to him, 'Look, why are they doing what is against the law on the Sabbath?'

Seeing this, the Pharisees alleged that by plucking and rubbing the corn the disciples were breaking another law, that of not working on the Sabbath. As they accosted Jesus about this, the Pharisees were not so much concerned for the Sabbath as their desire to obtain evidence with which they might discredit him.

2:25–26 He said to them, 'Have you never read what David did when he was in need and he and his companions were hungry — how he entered the house of God when Abiathar was high priest and ate the sacred bread, which is against the law for any but the priests to eat, and also gave it to his companions?'

Jesus turned the tables on the Pharisees by referring to an incident in the life of King David, whom they honoured as the greatest king Israel ever had; a man after God's own heart (1 Sam. 13:14). When David and his soldiers were fleeing from Saul on a Sabbath day, being very hungry they took and ate the sacred bread which had been consecrated and set before God as an offering. (The bread had only just been removed, which is how we know it was a Sabbath). Only the priests were allowed to eat this bread (Lev. 24:5–9). Therefore David broke the law. Jesus uses this as evidence that the law of love means that providing for genuine human need comes before the ceremonial law.

2:27 Then he said to them, 'The Sabbath was made for people, not people for the Sabbath.

The Pharisees had put many burdens upon the people by their rules and regulations (Matt. 23:4), and had twisted the purpose of the Sabbath as if man was made for the Sabbath instead of the Sabbath being given to man for his physical and spiritual good; an opportunity to rest from his labours and keep a holy day of worship to the Lord (Exodus 20:8, 34:21).

2:28 For this reason the Son of Man is lord even of the Sabbath.'

Jesus goes even further by stating that since the Sabbath was made for man and he is the Son of Man then he has "the absolute right to overrule the Sabbath if he wills, because of his person and work as God's representative man" (A. Cole).

Discussion Questions for Chapter 2

1. vv. 1–12. Why do you think that Jesus first said to the paralysed man "your sins are forgiven", before healing him?

2. vv. 13–17. Why do you think that the Pharisees complained about Jesus eating with tax collectors and sinners? Why were they wrong to do so?

3. vv. 18–20. According to Jesus, why were his disciples not fasting? When would they begin to fast?

4. vv. 18–22. What do you think Jesus is teaching in the parable of the wine skins?

5. vv. 23–28. Do you keep a Sabbath day? If so, in what ways do you observe it as a "holy day"?

You will find suggested answers to the study questions on pages 183–193.

Mark Chapter 3

Doing Good on the Sabbath

3:1 Then Jesus entered the synagogue again, and a man was there who had a withered hand.

It was Jesus' custom to attend the local synagogue; and on this occasion he met there a man with a withered hand.

3:2 They watched Jesus closely to see if he would heal him on the Sabbath, so that they could accuse him.

The Pharisees were there, scrutinising Jesus' every word and action; ready to pounce on him with an accusation. They only saw the man's handicap as an opportunity to bring charges against Jesus—they had no compassion for the man himself. Jesus on the other hand saw the man's need, and reached out to him in genuine compassion; whilst at the same time taking the opportunity to emphasise his teaching concerning the Sabbath.

3:3 So he said to the man who had the withered hand, 'Stand up among all these people.'

In calling the man to come forward in front of the whole congregation Jesus was challenging the man's faith.

3:4 Then he said to them, 'Is it lawful to do good on the Sabbath, or evil, to save a life or destroy it?' But they were silent.

Jesus then challenged his opponents by asking them "is it lawful to do good or evil on the Sabbath?" They did not dare answer him, for they did not wish to become ensnared in the very trap which they had set for him.

3:5 After looking around at them in anger, grieved by the hardness of their hearts, he said to the man, 'Stretch out your hand.' He stretched it out, and his hand was restored.

The Lord became very angry and was grieved over the hardness of their hearts; their unwillingness to bend the rules even for the sake of a helpless man. To the Hebrew "hardness of heart" meant "a stubborn resistance to the purpose of God" (A. Cole). If finding such hardness in the hearts of his enemies caused Christ pain, how much more must he be grieved to find hard hearts among the common people (John 12:37–40) or even his own disciples (Mark 6:52). At the command of Jesus the man stretched out his hand, and as he did so it was healed.

3:6 So the Pharisees went out immediately and began plotting with the Herodians, as to how they could assassinate him.

The Pharisees did not rejoice to see the man healed; they only saw Jesus as a threat to their authority and that of the Law of Moses. The Pharisees and the Herodians hated each other vehemently, yet such was their mutual hatred of Christ that they joined forces in order to plot his death.

Note: Herodians. These were a party among the Jews who were supporters of King Herod and his family, as they looked upon him as the last hope for the Jews of retaining their own national government, as distinguished from absolute dependence on Rome

3:7–8 Then Jesus went away with his disciples to the sea, and a great multitude from Galilee followed him. And from Judea, Jerusalem, Idumea, beyond the Jordan River, and around Tyre and Sidon a great multitude came to him when they heard about the things he had done.

Because of the rejection of the religious leaders Jesus withdrew from his synagogue ministry to continue preaching in the open air, as so many have been forced to do since (e.g. John Wesley in England). Christ returned to the seaside where the people came to him, not only from Galilee but from all over Israel. They came to hear his teaching and to be healed by him. The reason for the vast crowds was the publicity Jesus had gained by "word of mouth". They had heard from others the mighty things that Jesus had done, and wanted to see for themselves. It is only as we tell others about Jesus that they can know his power to save them (Rom. 10:14). Yet we also learn from these verses that there are times in our witnessing when we need to withdraw (as Christ did from the Pharisees) and allow the Holy Spirit to do his work, especially when our witness is rejected.

3:9 Because of the crowd, he told his disciples to have a small boat ready for him so the crowd would not press toward him.

The Lord was not ignorant of the possibility of his being overcome by the crush of the large crowd, and so asked his disciples to have a small boat standing by that he might use it as a pulpit. We might wonder why he should take this precaution, since in other places we see Christ divinely protected from the crowds (such as those who wanted to throw him over the cliff in Nazareth in Luke 4:29–30). Yet it appears that even in Jesus' case, God expects men to use their common sense, and if provision can be made, to make it. Remember what Jesus answered when Satan tempted him to throw himself from the pinnacle of the temple (Matt. 4:7).

3:10 For he had healed many, so that all who were afflicted with diseases pressed toward him in order to touch him.

There seemed to be no end to the number of people who needed healing of a huge variety of diseases. We read again that *many* were healed, which would perhaps suggest that not everybody was; not because of Christ's inability but because of their unbelief.

3:11–12 And whenever the unclean spirits saw him, they fell down before him and cried out, 'You are the Son of God.' But he sternly ordered them not to make him known.

Whenever unclean spirits saw him, they fell at his feet and cried out; acknowledging who he was. One commenter has suggested that the reason that there was such great activity by demonic power at this time was because Jesus Christ had come to destroy them. The reason for the increase in the manifestation of demonic power in the world today might be the same—for the devil and his demons know that the time is short before Christ comes to cast them into the lake of fire (Rev. 12:12; 20:10).

Christ silences the demons, for he does not need their testimony. What matters most to God is not the confession of vanquished demons, but the voluntary confession from the hearts of men who gladly yield their allegiance to him.

Jesus Calls the Twelve

3:13 Now Jesus went up the mountain and called for those he wanted, and they came to him.

Jesus next departed to the quietness of the mountains, where we are told that he prayed all night before choosing his twelve apostles (Luke 6:12–13). Like Jesus, before we make any important decision, we should pray and have an open heart to receive the answer; whatever it might be. We may not all have the privilege today of being called as apostles, but Jesus is continually calling every one of us to a closer walk with him.

3:14–15 He appointed twelve (whom he named apostles), so that they would be with him and he could send them to preach and to have authority to cast out demons.

Christ's purpose in choosing these men was to prepare them for the ministry he wanted them to fulfil. This ministry entailed preaching the gospel message and (through Christ's name) healing the sick and casting out demons.

3:16–19 He appointed twelve: To Simon he gave the name Peter; to James and his brother John, the sons of Zebedee, he gave the name Boanerges (that is, 'sons of thunder'); and Andrew, Philip, Bartholomew, Matthew, Thomas, James the son of Alphaeus, Thaddaeus, Simon the Zealot, and Judas Iscariot, who betrayed him.

The apostles were certainly a mixed bunch and if they were interviewed by employers according to today's values they certainly would not have been chosen for the job. But God does not look at the outward appearance, or at our achievements, but at the heart (1 Sam. 16:7).

Consider those who were chosen: Simon (meaning hasty, or rough and ready); whom he re-named Peter (a rock), for Jesus new that a work of grace would be done in his life to make him steadfast and sure; Andrew—the earnest but quiet witness who brought his brother Simon to the Lord (John 1:40–41); James and John—the sons of thunder, boisterous, demanding (Mark 10:35–36) and aggressive. You would never have thought that John would be found leaning on Jesus' breast and that James would be martyred so early in his ministry (Acts 12:1–2). Philip was slow to understand the truth (John 14:8), but he became an earnest witness. He found Nathanael (Bartholomew), who was a thinker, and in whom was no deceit. Matthew was the hated tax collector and cheat who worked for the Roman enemies. So-called "doubting" Thomas was also chosen, together with Judas Iscariot, the thief and betrayer. Of the other disciples named here we know very little.

Division

3:20–21 Now Jesus went home, and a crowd gathered so that they were not able to eat. When his family heard this they went out to restrain him, for they said, 'He is out of his mind.'

The family of Jesus did not believe in him until after the resurrection. On hearing that he was so heavily pressed by the people that neither he nor his disciples had time to even eat, they arrived to take him back home, accusing him of being mad.

3:22 The experts in the law who came down from Jerusalem said, 'He is possessed by Beelzebul,' and, 'By the ruler of demons he casts out demons.'

The scribes who had come especially from Jerusalem to trap him seized this opportunity to accuse Jesus of being possessed by the devil or a demon (Beelzebul) and of casting out demons by the power of the prince of the devils (Satan).

3:23 So he called them and spoke to them in parables: 'How can Satan cast out Satan?

Note that Jesus does not get angry or openly rebuke the lawyers, but calls them to him privately and corrects them by giving three parables. But first of all he asks them a simple and clear question: "how can Satan cast out Satan?"

3:24–25 If a kingdom is divided against itself, that kingdom will not be able to stand. If a house is divided against itself, that house will not be able to stand.

The first parable they should have understood from reference to their history in the Old Testament. A kingdom is united when it has one king to reign over it. Saul was the first king of Israel, David the second and Solomon the third. Only these three kings ruled over a united kingdom, for when Solomon died and his son Rehoboam became king the kingdom was divided. The two tribes of Judah and Benjamin became one kingdom under Rehoboam and the other ten tribes formed the northern kingdom, appointing their own king (Jeroboam). Eventually both kingdoms were destroyed and all the tribes were scattered throughout the world (1 Kings 12). The second parable of a house divided against itself is more personal, since if there is strife or rebellion in the family home it will not remain together.

3:26 And if Satan rises against himself and is divided, he is not able to stand and his end has come.

So it is with Satan: if he rose up in rebellion against himself, he could not stand but would bring about his own destruction.

3:27 But no one is able to enter a strong man's house and steal his property unless he first ties up the strong man. Then he can thoroughly plunder his house.

This third parable concerns the Lord's defeat of Satan. The strong man is the devil; his goods are those he holds captive by sin. He will not willingly give his goods over but will fight to retain them. The stronger man who comes to take his possessions is the Lord Jesus Christ who has bound the strong man and set the captives free (Isaiah 53:12; John 12:32; 2 Thess. 2:8; Heb. 2:14).

The Unpardonable Sin

3:28–30 I tell you the truth, people will be forgiven for all sins, even all the blasphemies they utter. But whoever blasphemes against the Holy Spirit will never be forgiven, but is guilty of an eternal sin' (because they said, 'He has an unclean spirit').

In these verses it is made quite clear that the unpardonable sin is attributing the work of the Holy Spirit to the devil; it is the sin of the wilfully blind. Jesus says that "all other sins will be forgiven" except this one and that those who commit it will be in danger of eternal condemnation.

Here is a word of warning: the devil loves to bind the people of God by convincing them that they have committed the unpardonable sin, but for anyone to commit this sin, they must have extremely hard heart, so as Selwyn Hughes writes: "any believer who claims to have committed the unpardonable sin is hardly likely to have done so for they would have no feeling of personal concern over the salvation of their soul, or manifest a serious desire to be forgiven".

The Relationship with Jesus

3:31–33 Then Jesus' mother and his brothers came. Standing outside, they sent word to him, to summon him. A crowd was sitting around him and they said to him, 'Look, your mother and your brothers are outside looking for you.' He answered them and said, 'Who are my mother and my brothers?'

The family of Jesus (his mother, brothers and sisters) again appeared on the scene. When told that they were outside looking for him, he looked around at the people gathered to listen to his teaching and asked who his mother and brothers were.

3:34–35 And looking at those who were sitting around him in a circle, he said, 'Here are my mother and my brothers! For whoever does the will of God is my brother and sister and mother.'

Christ's answer was that only those who do the will of God his Father could truly claim to be part of his family (John 1:12; 2 Cor. 6:18; Gal. 4:6). Since his own family did not believe in him at that time, they were not doing God's will and were not yet part of God's family. It is because we have a relationship with Jesus Christ that we are heirs of God and joint heir with Christ (Rom. 8:17). "Beloved, now we are children of God; and it has not yet been revealed what we shall be, but we know that when he is revealed, we shall be like him, for we shall see him as he is" (1 John 3:2).

In the end of the previous chapter we saw how the family of Jesus came to take him home. But Jesus refused to go, continuing instead with his Father's business (Luke 2:49) and withdrew for a time from his family. The Lord never asks any of his disciples to do what he was not prepared to do. In Matthew 10:37, he said, "He who loves or takes more pleasure in father, mother, son or daughter than in me is not worthy of me". We do not hear about Jesus' family again until we read of his mother being present at his crucifixion (John 19:26).

Discussion Questions for Chapter 3

1. vv.1–6. Here Jesus performs another miracle in front of the Pharisees. What do you think was the reason for their rejection of Christ in the face of such evidence?

2. vv. 13–19. Why do you think it was important for Jesus to pray before appointing the twelve apostles?

3. vv. 20–21. Can you think why Jesus' family thought that he was mad?

4. vv. 20–30. How and by whom can Satan be cast out?

5. vv. 31–33. Describe the characteristics of someone who is part of God's family.

You will find suggested answers to the study questions on pages 183–193.

Mark Chapter 4

4:1 Again he began to teach by the lake. Such a large crowd gathered around him that he got into a boat on the lake and sat there while the whole crowd was on the shore by the lake.

Here we find Jesus again at the seaside, this time sat in the boat, teaching the people, not by preaching, but by using parables.

What Parables are and their Purpose

4:2 He taught them many things in parables, and in his teaching said to them:

The common definition of a parable is that it is an earthly story with a heavenly meaning, but it is more correct to say that when Jesus took an everyday activity or common item and used it to explain a spiritual truth, then that is what we call a parable.

The Parable of the Sower and its Meaning

In this passage it might be easier to place Jesus' parable given in vv. 3–9 side by side with the explanation he later gave to his disciples in vv. 14–20.

4:3 'Listen! A sower went out to sow.

4:14 The sower sows the word.

The seed is the Word of God. In the first instance the sower is the Lord Jesus Christ; but he has since passed the responsibility for sowing God's word to all his followers (Mark 16:15). By his Spirit he enables them to carry out this responsibility (Acts 1:8). Although we may wonder at times why God's word is not as effective as it should be, it is not the seed that is at fault, as this parable clearly shows. The word of God is pure (Psalm 12:6) and sure (Luke 21:33). Every good gardener knows that if you want your seed to germinate then the ground has to be prepared properly first, and the soil needs to be good for it to produce abundantly. It is the ground that it is sown in is at fault if the seed fails to produce fruit.

4:4 And as he sowed, some seed fell along the path, and the birds came and devoured it.

4:15 These are the ones on the path where the word is sown: Whenever they hear, immediately Satan comes and snatches the word that was sown in them.

In Jesus' parable, the sower did not sow his seed sparingly from a packet but from a large basket; scattering it plentifully over the ground. As he did so some fell on uncultivated ground. This speaks of those who have a hardened heart. They hear the word but it goes no further than their ears. Like the birds come to eat the seed on the path, so Satan snatches away the word from unbelieving hearts (2 Cor. 4:4).

4:5–6 Other seed fell on rocky ground where it did not have much soil. It sprang up at once because the soil was not deep. When the sun came up it was scorched, and because it did not have sufficient root, it withered.

4:16–17 These are the ones sown on rocky ground: As soon as they hear the word, they receive it with joy. But they have no root in themselves and do not endure. Then, when trouble or persecution comes because of the word, immediately they fall away.

Some seed fell on rocky ground—these are the emotional hearers. They receive the word straight away with great joy and they seem to flourish for a while. But because they have not taken the word into their hearts when trouble comes and they are persecuted for the word's sake they fall away and are seen no more.

4:7 Other seed fell among the thorns, and they grew up and choked it, and it did not produce grain.

4:18–19 Others are the ones sown among thorns: They are those who hear the word, but worldly cares, the seductiveness of wealth, and the desire for other things come in and choke the word, and it produces nothing.

Then some fell among the thorns—these are the worldly hearers. They receive the word of God but are so tied up with the world that they never become separated from it. They continue to walk in the ways of the world and desire to fill themselves with it until the word is crowded out and there is no room for spiritual fruit to grow in them (see 1 John 2:15; Rom. 12:2).

4:8 But other seed fell on good soil and produced grain, sprouting and growing; some yielded thirty times as much, some sixty, and some a hundred times.

4:20 But these are the ones sown on good soil: They hear the word and receive it and bear fruit, one thirty times as much, one sixty, and one a hundred.'

Some seed fell on good ground—which stands for those with prepared and receptive hearts. These are the people who receive the word into the depths of their soul where it abides and matures. Such people grow in grace and in the knowledge of the Lord, and the fruit of the Spirit abounds in them.

This parable is generally applied to the sowing of the gospel message among the unconverted, but it is equally applicable to believers and the way in which they respond to the word of God. Jesus demands the attention of his hearers, in verse three he says "listen" and in verse nine he is saying if the Holy Spirit has opened your ears then you are now responsible for how you receive the word.

4:10 When he was alone, those around him with the twelve asked him about the parables.

Jesus had spoken this parable to the masses of people, but when his disciples were alone with him they asked why he spoke in parables.

4:11 He said to them, 'The secret of the kingdom of God has been given to you. But to those outside, everything is in parables,

To those who are Christ's followers and believe in him, the truth about the kingdom of God is clearly revealed. But to those who are outside, these spiritual truths remain hidden within the parables.

4:12 so that although they look they may look but not see, and although they hear they may hear but not understand, so they may not repent and be forgiven.'

This verse is a quote from Isaiah 6:9–10 which concerns Israel. Whilst Jesus' hearers may have understood the natural processes mentioned in the parable, they did not appreciate its spiritual application. Although they heard what was said they did not truly understand; for they did not want to. For if they should see and understand then they would no longer have an excuse for their wilful rejection of the truth which would otherwise have changed them and brought them to repentance and hence forgiveness. Such is the hardness of men's hearts. To put it another way "there are none as blind as those who will not see and none as deaf as those who will not hear".

Responsibility

Here Jesus explains the responsibility of those who have wholeheartedly received the word.

4:21 He also said to them, 'A lamp isn't brought to be put under a basket or under a bed, is it? Isn't it to be placed on a lampstand?

In the first instance this refers to the Lord Jesus Christ who came as the "light of the world". He did not come to hide himself but to reveal the Father, to be lifted up, like a lamp on a lampstand, that he might draw all men to himself (John 12:32). But as the light dwells in us we are to openly make our belief in Jesus known by our words and Christian behaviour.

4:22 For nothing is hidden except to be revealed, and nothing concealed except to be brought to light.

As light shows up everything so the Lord reveals the Father and all things concerning him.

4:23–24 If anyone has ears to hear, he had better listen!' And he said to them, 'Take care about what you hear. The measure you use will be the measure you receive, and more will be added to you.

Again he says "as the Holy Spirit has opened up your ears and understanding then pay careful attention to what you have heard." For each time we obey the truth which has been made known to us, God will reveal greater truth to us.

4:25 For whoever has will be given more, but whoever does not have, even what he has will be taken from him.'

The more we receive from God the more he will give to us; but if we are not faithful in the little that is given to us then even that will be taken away from us.

Spiritual Growth in the Individual Believer

4:26 He also said, 'The kingdom of God is like someone who spreads seed on the ground.

The fact that Jesus refers to this parable as one concerning the kingdom of God makes it clear that it is about those who have received the word into their hearts (1 John 2:14). The word "kingdom" refers to a territory or people over whom a king reigns therefore the kingdom of God refers to those who have willingly accepted the Lord Jesus Christ as king of their lives so that he reigns within their hearts (Luke 17:21; Eph. 3:17). The kingdom of God is within the church of Christ for he is the head of the church (Eph. 1:22). The kingdom is with us at the present time because it dwells within the heart of the believer. The kingdom is also to come when we are present with the Lord, when he comes to take his church to be where he is.

4:27 He goes to sleep and gets up, night and day, and the seed sprouts and grows, though he does not know how.

The word of God, having been sown, is left to grow within the heart. The farmer who goes about his daily business keeps an eye on the seed bed to see how the seeds are getting on but leaves nature to do its work. Thus the Lord keeps on eye on his own to make certain that everything is going according to his work of grace and to make certain that there is growth.

4:28 By itself the soil produces a crop, first the stalk, then the head, then the full grain in the head.

The Lord speaks here of the mystery of how a seed sown in the earth grows of its own accord. Man may sow the seed but it is God that causes it to grow and increase. So it is with spiritual growth; it is not brought about by our efforts but by the grace of God (1 Thess. 3:12). But we are to be willing and have a desire to grow in Christ (2 Pet. 3:18). Notice that it is not a sudden growth; it does not happen overnight like the seed sown on stony ground, but is gradual. First the blade—this is the first sign of something happening; the change that begins to take place in the believer's life which is visible to others. Then the ear—when more steps of faith are taken and a greater understanding of God's word and his ways are realized, until finally the full corn, the fullness of Christ is achieved (Eph. 4:13).

4:29 And when the grain is ripe, he sends in the sickle because the harvest has come.'

When we reach, or should I say, if we allow the Lord to bring us to full spiritual maturity, then he will gather us to himself, just as a farmer harvests his field when the corn is fully ripe. In this way Enoch who walked with God, when he reached the goal of spiritual maturity, did not see death but was transformed and transported to heaven (Gen. 5:24).

Spiritual Growth in the Church

4:30 He also asked, 'To what can we compare the kingdom of God, or what parable can we use to present it?

Jesus may have looked around to find another illustration to explain this next truth concerning the kingdom. Perhaps he caught sight of a mustard bush, and realised that the mustard seed would be ideal for his purpose.

4:31–32 It is like a mustard seed that when sown in the ground, even though it is the smallest of all the seeds in the ground — when it is sown, it grows up, becomes the greatest of all garden plants, and grows large branches so that the wild birds can nest in its shade.'

To start with the kingdom of God in comparison with other religions or philosophies was very small, like the mustard seed. Jesus had a very small band of followers compared with those who followed Judaism or the pagan gods. But when the small seed of the kingdom of God was sown it grew to become the largest of them all (Acts 5:14). Not only the largest but also it has spread its branches from Jerusalem and Judea to the uttermost parts of the world (Acts 1:8; Matt. 24:14; Rev. 14:6). The church of the Lord Jesus Christ has become a sanctuary and refuge to millions of people throughout the centuries and will continue to be so until Jesus comes. Just like the mustard bush became a dwelling for birds.

4:33–34 So with many parables like these, he spoke the word to them, as they were able to hear. He did not speak to them without a parable. But privately he explained everything to his own disciples.

Mark has here recorded only three of the many parables that Jesus told and that it was only by using parables that he taught the people; but later he explained everything to his disciples. Today the Lord does not need to speak to us by parables or to explain them for he has sent the Holy Spirit to teach us all things plainly in accordance with the truth (John 16:13).

Faith Tested

4:35 On that day, when evening came, Jesus said to his disciples, 'Let's go across to the other side of the lake.'

As the day drew to a close Jesus instructed the disciples to take the boat over to the other side of the Sea of Galilee. Jesus (who knows all things) was fully aware that a storm would arise, and yet still asked the disciples to launch out. The disciples themselves were completely ignorant of what lay ahead. There could not have been any sign of a storm approaching otherwise the fishermen would have argued against setting out. In a similar way, the Lord may direct us in paths that will test our faith and which we would not willingly take if we could foresee what lies ahead. Nevertheless like the disciples we must learn to do what Jesus says without questioning his reasons.

4:36 So after leaving the crowd, they took him along, just as he was, in the boat, and other boats were with him.

It is only in Mark's account of this event that we are told that there were other boats that accompanied the disciples on the Sea of Galilee. Often the experiences which we pass through in our Christian lives may affect others in a profound way.

4:37 Now a great windstorm developed and the waves were breaking into the boat, so that the boat was nearly swamped.

As often happens on the Sea of Galilee a storm arose quite suddenly; a wind storm with no rain attached to it. But it must have been of extraordinary force for it terrified even those disciples who were used to sudden storms. It was so fierce that it beat the waves into the boat so that it was on the verge of sinking. The testing of our faith may bring us where, like these disciples, we are almost overwhelmed and ready to give up hope.

4:38 But he was in the stern, sleeping on a cushion. They woke him up and said to him, 'Teacher, don't you care that we are about to die?'

Where was Jesus at this time? Apparently unaffected by the storm, he was still asleep and undisturbed by the waves that were rapidly filling the boat! The terrified disciples could not understand how he could be so unconcerned about their safety and so they woke him up and charged him with not caring about them. How often in the trials of our faith have we done the same, falsely accusing our Lord of not caring for our souls? The disciples should have known better; in the short time they had known Jesus they had witnessed many miracles of healing, deliverance and provision.

4:39 So he got up and rebuked the wind, and said to the sea, 'Be quiet! Calm down!' Then the wind stopped, and it was dead calm.

Jesus had been there in the boat all the time and knew very well what they were going through; yet he chose to wait until the disciples reached the limit of their endurance (1 Cor. 10:13). Once his purpose of developing and strengthening their trust was achieved, he immediately arose and rebuked the wind the sea and they both became calm. The disciples were saved and the people in the other boats on the sea were also rescued from the danger.

4:40 And he said to them, 'Why are you cowardly? Do you still not have faith?'

Having dealt with the elements he turned to his disciples and rebuked them for having fear because of their lack of faith.

4:41 They were overwhelmed by fear and said to one another, 'Who then is this? Even the wind and sea obey him!'

The fear that now came upon them was the right kind of fear, the awesome fear of God; for they realised when the wind and sea obeyed Jesus that he must be God manifest in the flesh.

Discussion Questions for Chapter 4

In chapter 4 Christ gives four parables on the subject of receiving the kingdom of God (which is synonymous with receiving Christ).

1. The Sower (vv.1–20)

What is the seed?

What does the seed produce when it is honestly received?

2. The Lamp (vv. 4:21–25)

How do you know when there is a lamp on in the room?

How can you tell when someone has genuinely received Christ?

What might the parable mean in terms of our witnessing for Christ?

3. The Seed Growing (vv. 26–29)

What does this parable tell us about the work of salvation?

4. The Mustard Seed (vv. 30–34)

The mustard seed is small but very effective, producing a tree large enough for birds to nest in. A tremendous change has happened to the mustard seed. How does this parable relate to those who receive Christ?

You will find suggested answers to the study questions on pages 183–193.

Mark Chapter 5

The Man of Gadara

5:1 So they came to the other side of the lake, to the region of the Gerasenes.

After the stilling of the storm, Jesus and his disciples arrived safely on the other side of the lake; in the region of the Gerasenes (or Gadara). Here they faced a storm of a different kind. In our Christian experience we find that no sooner are we delivered from one situation that we are faced with another.

5:2 Just as Jesus was getting out of the boat, a man with an unclean spirit came from the tombs and met him.

As soon as the boat reached the shore a man who was possessed by an unclean spirit came charging out of the nearby graveyard heading straight for Jesus.

5:3 He lived among the tombs, and no one could bind him anymore, not even with a chain.

This man's dwelling was among the dead; even as all outside of Christ are dead in their trespasses and sins (Prov. 21:16). Such was our condition in times past when we were bound by sin and the devil (Eph. 2:2–3). No one could control the forces of evil that drove this man; he could not even be restrained with chains.

5:4 For his hands and feet had often been bound with chains and shackles, but he had torn the chains apart and broken the shackles in pieces. No one was strong enough to subdue him.

The people had no spiritual answer to this man's spiritual condition, only a physical one and that was to try and restrain him with chains and fetters that proved to be useless. They were trying to fight the spiritual powers of darkness with the natural and found it was an impossible task (Eph. 6:12). They were trying to find a physical cure for a spiritual sickness and it did not work. The powers of darkness can only be fought by putting on the whole armour of God and by the spiritual weapons provided for us by the Lord Jesus Christ (Eph. 6:11–17). Only he is able to deliver and save.

5:5 Each night and every day among the tombs and in the mountains, he would cry out and cut himself with stones.

This man was not able to control himself because he was completely taken over by the unclean spirit who drove him into the mountains and among the graves as a restless tormented soul, "always shrieking, screaming, beating, bruising and cutting himself with stones." (Amp. N. T.) He would have eventually been driven to his death.

5:6 When he saw Jesus from a distance, he ran and bowed down before him.

Here is the all-important difference the man needed—Jesus came to him! As Jesus drew near the light of his glory and his power drew the man to him, in spite of the powers of darkness that possessed the man, and he fell down and worshiped him.

5:7 Then he cried out with a loud voice, 'Leave me alone, Jesus, Son of the Most High God! I implore you by God — do not torment me!'

From this verse to verse 12 the conversation is between Jesus and the chief demon that possessed the man. This demon confesses and acknowledges that Jesus is the Son of God for he could do none other for he knew that all power and authority had been given into the Lord's hand (Matt. 28:18). The demon asks "what is there in common between us?" The answer is nothing for they were entirely two opposites. The demon was unclean, unholy, characterised by darkness, and led by the Devil. Jesus is pure, holy, characterised by light, and is the Son of God—he did not need a demon to confess this. Surprisingly perhaps, this demon implores Jesus in the name of God not to torment him. The very presence of the Holy One caused him great distress and pain.

5:8 (For Jesus had said to him, 'Come out of that man, you unclean spirit!')

In Mark's account the demon cries out as Jesus is casting him out of the man but according to the following verses he did not leave until his request was granted. However in Matthew's account (Matt. 8:29–32) Jesus did not command that they leave the man until after their request. At the command of the Lord they had to obey.

5:9 Jesus asked him, 'What is your name?' And he said, 'My name is Legion, for we are many.'

For some reason Jesus questions this chief demon and asks his name which was Legion because he was the leader of the many demons who possessed the man. In the Roman army a legion comprised of anything between three to six thousand men.

5:10 He begged Jesus repeatedly not to send them out of the region.

The demon knew that he, along with his many companions, had to leave the man but they did not want to leave the region. This says quite a lot about this area as being a place of darkness where Satan's forces were very much at home and perhaps made to feel very much at home. So they kept on begging Jesus not to send them away from the area.

5:11–12 There on the hillside, a great herd of pigs was feeding. And the demonic spirits begged him, 'Send us into the pigs. Let us enter them.'

There was a large herd of swine at hand, that should not have been there because the pig was classed as an unclean animal in the law of God (Lev. 11:7). This fact again speaks of the nature of the people of the area.

(There are two suggestions given regarding the keeping of the pigs in Israel: that it was an area that Gentiles lived in and thus it was these who owned the pigs; and that they belong to Jews who bred them to sell to the Gentiles. Whichever may be correct, they should not have been there). As children of God we should make sure that we keep nothing in our lives or homes that could be used as channels or instruments for the devil to use (see Acts 19:19).

5:13 Jesus gave them permission. So the unclean spirits came out and went into the pigs. Then the herd rushed down the steep slope into the lake, and about two thousand were drowned in the lake.

No demon when faced with the power and authority of the Lord Jesus Christ can do what it chooses; he has to give them permission. They knew this and so does their master the Devil who is a defeated foe (Heb. 2:14). Jesus permitted them to go into the herd of swine that they immediately send charging to their death in the lake. This incident seems to suggest that demons need to possess living things in order to carry out their destructive purposes. Some commentators have suggested that when the pigs died the demons would have been bound in the dead pigs and therefore could do no more harm—but this statement borders on the ridiculous.

5:14 Now the herdsmen ran off and spread the news in the town and countryside, and the people went out to see what had happened.

The swineherds who saw all this happening fled in fear telling everybody they met what had occurred.

5:15 They came to Jesus and saw the demon-possessed man sitting there, clothed and in his right mind — the one who had the 'Legion' — and they were afraid.

On hearing this the people go to where Jesus and the man were staying and to their astonishment they find the man whom they could not

57

hold with fetters and chains sat meekly at the feet of Jesus. He, who had gone about naked, was now fully clothed; he whom the demons had tormented and driven to wander in the mountains among the graves was now sitting peacefully in his right mind talking with Jesus. This man was in fact a "new man", a "new creation" (2 Cor. 5:17). We cannot fail to see in this event the similarity of experience of the sinner who is bound by the world, the flesh and the devil, being set free and clothed in robes of righteousness by the Lord Jesus Christ. The people became afraid of what they saw, since they could not understand it.

5:16–18 Those who had seen what had happened to the demon-possessed man reported it, and they also told about the pigs. Then they asked Jesus to leave their region. As he was getting into the boat the man who had been demon-possessed asked if he could go with him.

When they had heard the full story from the swineherds their reaction was to beg Jesus, not to stay and show them the mighty works of God or to set them free, but to leave their area; which he did for he never forces his presence on anyone. The man who had been delivered naturally wanted to go with Jesus after all that he had done for him.

5:19 But Jesus did not permit him to do so. Instead, he said to him, 'Go to your home and to your people and tell them what the Lord has done for you, that he had mercy on you.'

But Jesus would not allow this, for he had other work for the man. Although the people had begged Jesus to leave them, he did not completely abandon them for he told the man to go back to his friends and tell them how much the Lord had done for him and how he had compassion and mercy upon him.

5:20 So he went away and began to proclaim in the Decapolis what Jesus had done for him, and all were amazed.

And the man did as the Lord commanded him. We are told that the people were amazed and marvelled at the man's testimony but it does not say that they believed and received the Lord Jesus Christ as their Saviour.

Jairus' Daughter and the Woman with the Issue of Blood

5:21 When Jesus had crossed again in a boat to the other side, a large crowd gathered around him, and he was by the sea.

This disciples and Jesus crossed back over the Sea of Galilee, this time without any trouble, and crowds of people again gathered to him.

5:22 Then one of the synagogue rulers, named Jairus, came up, and when he saw Jesus, he fell at his feet.

The first of the two people needing help from Jesus when he arrived was named Jairus. He was a ruler of the synagogue and may even have been a member of the ruling body, the Sanhedrin. Therefore it was no light matter for him to come seeking out Jesus for he knew his fellows members hated and were plotting to get rid of him. It cost him a great deal to come and humble himself before the Lord, falling down before him in worship. In falling at his feet he was acknowledging Jesus as his Lord, or certainly as someone who was far above his own standing in life.

5:23 He asked him urgently, 'My little daughter is near death. Come and lay your hands on her so that she may be healed and live.'

He further humbled himself in confessing his need of help to the point of earnestly begging Jesus to come to his house and lay his hands on his daughter who had a sickness unto death. He did not count the cost of losing his position in life or of being thrown off the Sanhedrin and out of the synagogue. He had no doubt whatsoever that Jesus was able and that he would heal his daughter. Such faith!

5:24 Jesus went with him, and a large crowd followed and pressed around him.

The Lord had compassion upon the man and immediately went with Jairus followed by the crowd.

5:25 Now a woman was there who had been suffering from a haemorrhage for twelve years.

Somewhere along the way a woman who had suffered with a continual loss of blood for over twelve years caught up with Jesus.

5:26 She had endured a great deal under the care of many doctors and had spent all that she had. Yet instead of getting better, she grew worse.

This woman had become poverty stricken by spending all that she had seeking a cure from the doctors; but all to no avail for instead of getting better she grew worse. In such extremity of human weakness, God has an opportunity to help.

5:27 When she heard about Jesus, she came up behind him in the crowd and touched his cloak,

On hearing about the many miracles of healing that Jesus had performed, faith arose in her heart. Although she had not seen these miracles for herself, she believed that if she could only reach him and touch his clothes she would be healed.

5:28 for she kept saying, 'If only I touch his clothes, I will be healed.'

Jairus believed that if the Lord touched his daughter she would be healed. The women believed if she could only touch his clothes she would be healed. Such faith! The woman would have come behind Jesus in order to touch him for she did not want to be seen. The sickness she had was classed as ceremonially unclean by the law, just like leprosy, and she was not allowed to have fellowship in the synagogue.

5:29 At once the bleeding stopped, and she felt in her body that she was healed of her disease.

As soon as she touched his garment she felt in her body that the flow of blood had stopped and that she was completely healed. This would seem to be one case when feelings could be counted on as proof of faith being fulfilled.

5:30 Jesus knew at once that power had gone out from him. He turned around in the crowd and said, 'Who touched my clothes?'

The woman thought that what she had done would go unnoticed especially as there were so many people about. But Jesus knew immediately that faith had reached out and touched him and that power had gone from him. He looked around and asked who had done this. This was not because he did not know, but because he wanted the woman to confess so that he could give her the word of assurance that she was indeed healed and that the disease would never come back to her.

5:31–32 His disciples said to him, 'You see the crowd pressing against you and you say, 'Who touched me?'' But he looked around to see who had done it.

The disciples could hardly believe their ears, considering the number of people who were around him and who were touching him. They seemingly could not understand the difference of a touch of faith and the casual touch of someone just brushing against Jesus.

5:33 Then the woman, with fear and trembling, knowing what had happened to her, came and fell down before him and told him the whole truth.

The woman was filled with terror at being found out. It was not enough to believe in the heart: the woman must also confess with her mouth (Rom. 10:9). It cost a great deal to do so, for she had to tell him her whole story before all the people.

5:34 He said to her, 'Daughter, your faith has made you well. Go in peace, and be healed of your disease.'

But she need not have feared. In fact like so many of our fears we need not have them. Jesus spoke comfort to her, revealing that the reason for her healing was her faith in him. She was not only healed but she received his peace and assurance of complete and permanent healing.

5:35–36 While he was still speaking, people came from the synagogue ruler's house saying, 'Your daughter has died. Why trouble the teacher any longer?' But Jesus, paying no attention to what was said, told the synagogue ruler, 'Do not be afraid; just believe.'

By this time Jairus must have begun to worry about his daughter and what this delay could mean; sure enough, messengers came from his home to tell him that his daughter had died, and that he should not bother Jesus any longer. His faith waned and fear took over, for fear is the opposite of faith and when fear comes in faith goes out. That is why there are so many exhortations from the Lord not to fear (Isaiah 43:1–3). When he heard the news what was Jairus' reaction? What would our reaction have been? Should he blame the woman for what had happened because she caused the delay?

Whatever his reactions might have been, Jesus was quick to reassure him that there was nothing to fear; he encouraged him to "only believe".

5:37 He did not let anyone follow him except Peter, James, and John, the brother of James.

From this point on Jesus stopped the crowd from following him and chose three of his disciples to go further with him. From the gospels we see that Peter, James and John were the disciples who desired to walk close with Jesus and their desire was rewarded by Jesus involving them more in his ministry (e.g. in the garden of Gethsemane).

5:38 They came to the house of the synagogue ruler where he saw noisy confusion and people weeping and wailing loudly.

When they arrived at the house it was not an encouraging sight that met them. From the weeping and wailing it was evident that the child had definitely died

5:39 When he entered he said to them, 'Why are you distressed and weeping? The child is not dead but asleep.'

The words of Jesus must have absolutely astounded the mourners. What was wrong with the man, did he not realise that death had visited the home? What did he know; he had not been there to see the dying moments of the child; asleep not dead? What nonsense! How often in different situations do we thus reason within ourselves and with the Lord?

5:40 And they began making fun of him. But he put them all outside and he took the child's father and mother and his own companions and went into the room where the child was.

How quickly their grief, weeping and wailing turned to laughter and mockery. Because of this and their unbelief they were excluded from going in with him and from the opportunity of witnessing a miracle. Only the father, mother and the three disciples were allowed to observe Jesus' power over death.

5:41–42 Then, gently taking the child by the hand, he said to her, 'Talitha koum,' which means, 'Little girl, I say to you, get up.' The girl got up at once and began to walk around (she was twelve years old). They were completely astonished at this.

Jesus did not do as Jairus had requested of him; that was, to lay his hands upon his daughter. So often the Lord does not answer our requests in the way we ask him to for his ways are not our ways and his thoughts are not our thoughts (Isaiah 55:8). Jesus gently takes her hand in his, as you would of a child that was alive, and speaks to her in her own native language. Immediately she rose from the dead and walked about to prove it. Mark points out that she was twelve years old and therefore of the age of understanding. It is obvious from the reaction of those present that they were not expecting to see the miracle of the dead being raised although they had earlier believed for healing. Jairus only had faith to believe that Jesus was able to heal the living—it did not stretch to believing that with God all things are possible; death is no obstacle to him.

5:43 He strictly ordered that no one should know about this, and told them to give her something to eat.

Why did Jesus command them not to tell anyone about what had happened? Surely they would find out soon enough. Before the miracle, those outside did not want to know, they were full of unbelief and had mocked, and by so doing they had excluded themselves from not only witnessing the miracle but also in participating in the joy of it.

Discussion Questions for Chapter 5

1. vv.1–15. What impresses you most about how Jesus delivered the man of Gadara?

2. vv. 16–17. Why do you think the people of Gadara asked Jesus to leave their region?

3. vv. 18–20. What was the impact of this man's witness to the people of Decapolis?

4. vv. 21–43. Why do you think it was difficult for Jairus to come to Jesus? What made him finally do it?

5. vv. 25–34. What lessons might we learn from the faith of the woman with the issue of blood?

You will find suggested answers to the study questions on pages 183–193.

Mark Chapter 6

Rejection

6:1 Now Jesus left that place and came to his hometown, and his disciples followed him.

Jesus then left the area where he had done so many miracles and returned to the area in which he was brought up; to his home town of Nazareth. He was often referred to as "Jesus of Nazareth" although he was born in Bethlehem, his family's ancestral home. Nazareth was however the home town of Joseph and Mary. We are told in Matthew 2:23 that it was foreordained that Jesus should live in Nazareth and thus be called a Nazarene. When Paul was brought before Felix the Jews accused him of being a member of the sect called the "Nazarenes" (Acts 24:5). This is what some called the followers of Jesus. Mark makes a point of the fact that the disciples followed him. This is significant in as much as they were all from the area that Jesus had up to this point worked in. Now they had to decide whether to stay with their families and friends or go with him to an unfamiliar area. They chose to follow Jesus.

6:2 When the Sabbath came, he began to teach in the synagogue. Many who heard him were astonished, saying, 'Where did he get these ideas? And what is this wisdom that has been given to him? What are these miracles that are done through his hands?

If anyone wanted to find Jesus on the Sabbath day they knew where to look during the service times—in the synagogue. He would have only read and taught from the scriptures at the invitation of the synagogue rulers; he would not have done so of his own accord. These people had regularly been taught by other rabbis from the scriptures but never before had they heard any speak like Jesus did "for he taught them as one having authority and not as the scribes" (Matt. 7:29). Yet it would seem that they were not so much amazed at what he had said as how a man, whom they had known from a child and whose only schooling would have been the little he had received at the synagogue had this wisdom, he the power from to do such mighty miracles that they had heard about!

6:3 Isn't this the carpenter, the son of Mary and brother of James, Joses, Judas, and Simon? And aren't his sisters here with us?' And so they took offense at him.

Their lack of knowledge and understanding brought remarks of contempt from them as to his lowly station in life "only a carpenter's son". His mother and his family still lived among them and were but common people. They were not prepared to accept him as the "Son of God" in spite of the proof that was presented before them, neither did they want to accept him as a man whom God had taken a hold of and empowered to be a prophet—just because they knew him and his lowly background so well. They were ignorant of the ways of God and of whom he chooses (1 Cor. 1:27–29). They were "offended" or correctly he became a stumbling block to them (1 Pet. 2:7–8).

6:4 Then Jesus said to them, 'A prophet is not without honor except in his hometown, and among his relatives, and in his own house.'

So Jesus quotes an old saying "a prophet is honoured in all countries but in his own and among relatives and in his own house he is rejected". If our Lord was so treated can we expect any better treatment?

6:5 He was not able to do a miracle there, except to lay his hands on a few sick people and heal them.

Because of their rejection and unbelief he could not do any miracles there except to heal a few who had faith enough to receive.

6:6 And he was amazed because of their unbelief. Then he went around among the villages and taught.

Now it was the Lord's turn to be amazed and this was at their unbelief, their lack of faith. He left Nazareth and we are not told that he ever visited it again. Instead he went to other towns and villages in the area. It is unbelief that stops the hand of God from moving.

Sending Forth

6:7 Jesus called the twelve and began to send them out two by two. He gave them authority over the unclean spirits.

In Mark 1:14 we saw that Jesus called the twelve disciples to be with at all times so that he might teach and prepare them to go forth to preach.

Now we see him sending them out for some practical experience of what he was been preparing them for. We could liken it in today's world of someone being on employment training and being sent out on placement to put into practice what they have learnt. He calls them to him and gives them precise instructions about how to do the job.

They must not go alone but in pairs, so that they may be company for each other; that they may strengthen the hands, encourage the hearts and be a help to each other (M. Henry). This is a rule that we should apply to our evangelism; we should not go it alone when we are sent into the highways and byways. (Personal witness, when a one to one as opportunity is given, is of course a different matter to being sent on a mission). He "gave" them power and authority over unclean spirits. It may be more correct to say that he loaned them this for the period that they were sent out, for apart from when he sent out the seventy (Luke 10:1–20), we do not hear of the disciples doing any further miracles until after Pentecost.

6:8 He instructed them to take nothing for the journey except a staff — no bread, no bag, no money in their belts

They were to travel light, taking with them a stick to help them walk, no food, no money, for they were to prove the Lord as the one who provides.

6:9 and to put on sandals but not to wear two tunics.

They were to wear sandals, in readiness to travel and preach (this reminds us of part of the armour of God in Eph. 6:5, a readiness to preach) and only one coat which suggests that it was either summer or harvest time.

6:10 He said to them, 'Wherever you enter a house, stay there until you leave the area.

If they were offered hospitality in a home they were to remain in that place for as long as they were in the town and not go from house to house, as this could cause offence to the first person who had freely taken them in.

6:11 If a place will not welcome you or listen to you, as you go out from there, shake the dust off your feet as a testimony against them.'

If they were not received or welcomed in any community and if their message was not listened to, they were to leave it. As they left that place, as a symbolic act, they were to shake off the dust of that place from their feet as a witness against them of their rejection (see Acts 13:50–51). Mark does not have the closing words of Jesus to the disciples in Matthew's version "it will be more tolerable for Sodom and Gomorrah in the day of judgement"; words which suggest that there will be various degrees of punishment for unbelievers (Matt. 11:22).

6:12 So they went out and preached that all should repent.

And so the disciples were sent forth and followed Jesus' instructions to the letter, preaching the gospel to the people calling on them to repent.

6:13 They cast out many demons and anointed many sick people with oil and healed them.

And because they did as he instructed them their ministry prospered, and many were delivered from demons. Although we are not told in the preceding verses that Jesus instructed them, nevertheless he must have done so, for as they anointed the sick with oil they were healed (James 5:14).

In between the time of the disciples being sent out (verse 7) and their returning to Jesus (verse 30) Mark fills us in on what became of John the Baptist.

6:14–15 Now King Herod heard this, for Jesus' name had become known. Some were saying, "John the baptizer has been raised from the dead, and because of this, miraculous powers are at work in him." Now King Herod heard this, for Jesus' name had become known. Some were saying, "John the baptizer[21] has been raised from the dead, and because of this, miraculous powers are at work in him."

The miracles that Jesus was doing reached the ears of King Herod and it pricked his conscience; for he immediately thought that John the Baptist had been raised from the dead. From his reaction we can assume that Herod had no difficulty in believing in resurrection and that if anyone could be raised from the dead then the matter of miracles would be a natural consequence of this. Others thought that it was Elijah come back and some that at least he must be one of the prophets.

6:16–18. But when Herod heard this, he said, "John, whom I beheaded, has been raised!" Herod himself had sent men, arrested John, and bound him in prison on account of Herodias, his brother Philip's wife, because Herod[22] had married her. For John had repeatedly told Herod, "It is not lawful for you to have your brother's wife."

Herod was convinced that it was none other than John. The reason why Herod had John imprisoned was because he had repeatedly and boldly declared the truth that he was committing sin by marrying his brother Philip's wife Herodias.

6:19–20 So Herodias nursed a grudge against him and wanted to kill him. But she could not because Herod stood in awe of John and protected him, since he knew that John was a righteous and holy man. When Herod heard him, he was thoroughly baffled, and yet he liked to listen to John.

Therefore, Herodias was enraged with John and held a grudge against him but she could not carry out her revenge because Herod had a fear of John. He knew that he was a just and holy man, and this was why he had up to now protected John from the evil plans and purposes of his unlawful wife. Although what John said disturbed him, Herod still liked to listen to him.

6:21 But a suitable day came, when Herod gave a banquet on his birthday for his court officials, military commanders, and leaders of Galilee.

However, when it was Herod's birthday party and all the high dignitaries were there, Herodias seized an opportunity to get her own back on John.

6:22. (NKJV™) And when Herodias' daughter herself came in and danced, and pleased Herod and those who sat with him, the king said to the girl, "Ask me whatever you want, and I will give it to you." He also swore to her, "Whatever you ask me, I will give you, up to half my kingdom."

During the festivities Herodias' daughter came and danced before all the guests and because this greatly pleased Herod he rashly promised her on oath to give her whatever she wanted—even up to half his kingdom.

6:24 So she went out and said to her mother, "What shall I ask?" And she said, "The head of John the Baptist!"

The daughter, who was obviously ruled by her mother, went straight to her and asked what she should ask for. This was Herodias' chance and she did not hesitate to say the execution of John the Baptist.

6:25–26 Immediately she hurried back to the king and made her request: "I want the head of John the Baptist on a platter immediately." Although it grieved the king deeply, he did not want to reject her request because of his oath and his guests.

So the girl returned to the king and told him she wanted the head of John the Baptist presented to her on a plate. Although he deeply regretted what he had said he could not refuse her request because of the oath he had made before all his guests.

6:27–28 So the king sent an executioner at once to bring John's head, and he went and beheaded John in prison. He brought his head on a platter and gave it to the girl, and the girl gave it to her mother.

Just as Ahab listened to Jezebel (1 Kings 21:25) so Herod yielded to his wife and by making a rash oath to her daughter he put himself in the position of doing what he knew was wrong. John the Baptist was executed.

We should be very careful concerning any oaths that we might make, especial those we make to God. They should be considered very carefully and not made on the spur of the moment.

6:29 When John's disciples heard this, they came and took his body and placed it in a tomb.

When John's disciples heard about this they came and took his body and buried it in a tomb.

Miracle of Provision

6:30 Then the apostles gathered around Jesus and told him everything they had done and taught.

On their return to Jesus, the disciples were very eager to tell him all that they had done and said during their evangelistic tour. They were as excited about it as children would have been to report the results of a project they had successfully completed for their teacher. However, keep in mind the exuberance of the disciples when they returned to Jesus from their successful evangelistic outreach is placed in contrast their utter helplessness and lack of faith in responding to his challenge to feed 5,000 people as well as their fear when he came to them walking on the water.

6:31 He said to them, "Come with me privately to an isolated place and rest a while" (for many were coming and going, and there was no time to eat).

The Lord saw that the work had taken its toll on his disciples and that they were in need of a rest. There are times when the Lord calls us aside for a while that we might wait upon Him and be renewed in strength (Isaiah 40:31).

6:32 So they went away by themselves in a boat to some remote place.

So He apparently planned a little quiet holiday for them away from the crowds, although Jesus was never taken unawares and knew what was about to happen.

6:33 But many saw them leaving and recognized them, and they hurried on foot from all the towns and arrived there ahead of them.

Many of the people recognized who they were and when they saw them getting into a boat they rushed round to the other side of the lake and met them there.

6:34 As Jesus came ashore he saw the large crowd and he had compassion on them, because they were like sheep without a shepherd. So he taught them many things.

When Jesus looked upon the people he saw them as lost sheep having no shepherd to protect, provide or guide them (Isaiah 53:6; Jer. 50:6, Ezek. 34:6). As much as his disciples needed a rest, the needs of the people were greater; so being moved with compassion he could not turn them away, but instead ministered to them. Who else did they have to turn to but him? (Ps.23:1; Isaiah 40:11; John 10:11)

6:35–36 When it was already late, his disciples came to him and said, "This is an isolated place and it is already very late. Send them away so that they can go into the surrounding countryside and villages and buy something for themselves to eat."

Perhaps by now the disciples were feeling a bit put-out since they had lost out on a day's holiday. They wanted to get rid of the people as soon as they could; so when they saw it was getting late they asked Jesus to send them away that they might find themselves some food to eat.

6:37 (NKJV™) But He answered and said to them, "You give them something to eat." And they said to Him, "Shall we go and buy two hundred denarii worth of bread and give them something to eat?"

Imagine their surprise when he turned round and told them to feed the crowds! After all, he had provided for them on their recent evangelistic journey when they took no provisions with them. It was time to stretch their faith even further and trust God to provide for others. However, their faith failed and they could only ask Jesus in amazement if they should go and buy 200 denarii of bread to feed the people. Did they miss an opportunity of seeing a miracle performed through their faith and by their own hands?

6:38. He said to them, "How many loaves do you have? Go and see." When they found out, they said, "Five — and two fish."

Jesus then offered them a challenge, asking, "What have you already got?" They had nothing worth talking about; just five loaves and a couple of fish. It seemed like nothing to the disciples but in the hands of the

73

Lord Jesus Christ it was enough. When God spoke to Moses from out of the burning bush he asked "What is that in your hand?" It was only a piece of wood (a rod)—but it was enough for God to use. We may complain to the Lord about the little that we may have to work for him but he does not ask us if we have enough; he asks us about what we *have* got. Whatever we put into his hands, he is able to do mighty things with it.

6:39–40 Then he directed them all to sit down in groups on the green grass. So they reclined in groups of hundreds and fifties.

Our God is always a God of order and never of confusion (1 Cor. 14:33) for in the beginning when He created the heavens and the earth he made order out of chaos. Jesus made sure that the people were sitting in orderly rows and made comfortable.

6:41–44 He took the five loaves and the two fish, and looking up to heaven, he gave thanks and broke the loaves. He gave them to his disciples to serve the people, and he divided the two fish among them all. They all ate and were satisfied, and they picked up the broken pieces and fish that were left over, twelve baskets full. Now there were five thousand men who ate the bread.

Then he took the bread and fish, asking the blessing on them. As they were distributed to the people so the miracle of provision took place and above 5,000 were adequately fed and there was even a basketful of fragments left over for each one of the disciples. So despite their unbelief, by the grace of the Lord, the disciples did have a hand in the miracle.

Miracle of walking on water

6:45 Immediately Jesus made his disciples get into the boat and go on ahead to the other side, to Bethsaida, while he dispersed the crowd.

As soon as the disciples had finished collecting the left overs Jesus packed them off in the ship to Bethsaida (which means house of fish) for their rest (Amp. N.T. says that he insisted they go) while he sent the crowd away having been fully fed spiritually and physically.

6:46–47 After saying good-bye to them, he went to the mountain to pray. When evening came, the boat was in the middle of the sea and he was alone on the land.

Having done this, Jesus went up into the mountain alone to pray. When the evening had come the boat was in the middle of the lake and Jesus was on the land by himself.

6:48 He saw them straining at the oars, because the wind was against them. As the night was ending, he came to them walking on the sea, for he wanted to pass by them.

The disciples were not conscious of him but he was very mindful of them, for he saw that they were in trouble, having difficulty in rowing because the wind was against them. This was a different situation to the time when they were on the lake at the mercy of the storm. They were afraid then even though Jesus was with them, but this time they were struggling in the hardness and difficulty of the way and Jesus was nowhere to be seen. Little did they know that he was aware of the problems they were having and yet he deliberately delayed his coming.

We who are this side of the cross know by faith that Jesus is ever present with us, for he has promised never to leave us or forsake us (Heb. 13:5, Matt. 28:20). In the fourth watch of the night, when he knew that they could not endure any longer, he came to them (1 Cor. 10:13). Certainly, not in a way they expected him to come; but walking on the water! Similarly today, Jesus often comes to our help in ways that we do not expect, and if perhaps later than we had hoped, he is still on time.

6:49. When they saw him walking on the water they thought he was a ghost. They cried out,

Fear took a hold of them as they saw this figure walking towards them over the water and they cried out in terror! What else could they think but that it was a ghost for no one had ever walked on water before—it was impossible!

6:50. for they all saw him and were terrified. But immediately he spoke to them: "Have courage! It is I. Do not be afraid."

When Jesus saw how terrified they were, he called out to them, "Take heart! I AM! Stop being alarmed and afraid" (Amp. N. T.). The Amplified New Testament here notes that Jesus used his Divine Name—"I AM."

6:51–52. Then he went up with them into the boat, and the wind ceased. They were completely astonished, because they did not understand about the loaves, but their hearts were hardened.

They were calmed by recognising his voice and by the words that he spoke. When he entered the ship the wind dropped. This shows again that this was a time of testing for the disciples. They were completely amazed by all of this because they had not understood the teaching and meaning of the miracle of feeding the 5,000—that he was Lord of all! His own disciples had become hardened, so no wonder he allowed them to go through this time of testing! The truth would only sink in through the hardness of the way—how much easier it would be for all of us if we learnt our lessons the first time!

Change of Attitude

6:53. After they had crossed over, they came to land at Gennesaret and anchored there.

Jesus now returns to the area of Gennesaret where he had delivered the man from the Legion of demons and where the people who kept the pigs had begged him to leave the area.

6:54–55 As they got out of the boat, people immediately recognized Jesus. They ran through that whole region and began to bring the sick on mats to wherever he was rumored to be.

The man whom Jesus had set free had done a good job of witnessing (Mark 5:20) for hundreds of people flocked to him from all the towns and villages of the area so that they might be healed.

6:56 And wherever he would go — into villages, towns, or countryside — they would place the sick in the marketplaces, and would ask him if they could just touch the edge of his cloak, and all who touched it were healed.

They may have also heard of the woman with the issue of blood who touch the hem of His garment for they also desired to do the same thing to receive healing. What a change of attitude they had towards Jesus from his previous visit! But the Lord is good and ready to forgive and plenteous in mercy to all those who call on Him (Psalm 86:5).

Discussion Questions for Chapter 6

1. vv. 7–13. When the Lord Jesus called his apostles to himself, what did he send them to do?

2. vv. 14–29. What did it cost John to remain a faithful witness to Jesus Christ?

3. vv. 30–33. How do you think the apostles felt when they finished the work Jesus gave them?

4. vv. 34–44. What can the feeding of the 5,000 teach us about serving Christ?

5. Read again about the miracles in vv.45–52 and vv. 53–56 and comment briefly on each one.

You will find suggested answers to the study questions on pages 183–193.

Mark Chapter 7

A Form of Godliness

7:1 Now the Pharisees and some of the experts in the law who came from Jerusalem gathered around him.

The fame of Jesus had spread as far as Jerusalem and the reports of his teaching, more than his miracles, disturbed the chief priest and the religious rulers. So they sent a contingent of Pharisees and scribes, who represented the Law and laid great stress not on the righteousness of an action, but upon its formal correctness, to find out exactly what he was teaching the people. They did not come with open hearts or minds; they had already judged the Lord and came with a criticising spirit. Such a spirit, if found in a church, can hinder the work of God and has been the downfall of many a righteous man (see 2 Cor. 8:20; Acts 11:2–3 NIV).

7:2 And they saw that some of Jesus' disciples ate their bread with unclean hands, that is, unwashed.

That is why these spies, for that is what they were, when they saw Jesus' disciples eating without washing their hands, criticized them in order to get at Jesus. For if, as their teacher, he allowed them to do this kind of thing then he must have been doing the same.

7:3–4 (For the Pharisees and all the Jews do not eat unless they perform a ritual washing, holding fast to the tradition of the elders. And when they come from the marketplace, they do not eat unless they wash. They hold fast to many other traditions: the washing of cups, pots, kettles, and dining couches.)

They expected everybody to act as they did, according to their rules and regulations which were additions to the Law of God that had been handed down by their forefathers. It was not for hygienic reasons that they washed their hands, or the other items mentioned; the washing was merely ceremonial.

7:5 The Pharisees and the experts in the law asked him, 'Why do your disciples not live according to the tradition of the elders, but eat with unwashed hands?'

They kept on asking Jesus why his disciples did not keep these traditions.

7:6–7 He said to them, 'Isaiah prophesied correctly about you hypocrites, as it is written: 'This people honours me with their lips, but their heart is far from me. They worship me in vain, teaching as doctrine the commandments of men.'

Jesus knew their hearts and that they had a form of true religion but denied and rejected the power of it and thus he quoted to them from Isaiah 29:13. If we are called to give an answer to anyone it is far better to quote from scripture (not necessarily the actual words, although it is better if we can, but the correct meaning of them) than to try to from our own knowledge and our own words.

He called them pretenders and hypocrites (playing at being religious) for although praised and exalted God with their mouths, their hearts are hardened and they were actually far away from him (2 Tim. 3:5). Their worship was useless because it was not acceptable to God; they did not worship in spirit and truth (Phil. 3:3). Instead they went about teaching the commands of men.

7:8 Having no regard for the command of God, you hold fast to human tradition.

They despised the word of God and in fact rejected it in preference for rules invented by men. In doing this they were placing a heavy burden on the people, more than they could bear, and more than God demanded. In contrast, Jesus could say in Matthew 11:30 "my burden is light", for he did not come to place a burden on us but to take our burdens away.

7:9 He also said to them, 'You neatly reject the commandment of God in order to set up your tradition.

The Pharisees rejected and discouraged people from following God's word in order to keep their own tradition. In the next few verses Jesus gives an example of this.

Honor Parents

7:10 For Moses said, 'Honor your father and your mother,' and, 'Whoever insults his father or mother must be put to death.'

He quotes from a number of scriptures (Ex. 20:12; Ex. 21:17). God considers it very important that this command should be obeyed, to honour—that is, respect with tenderness of feeling—and obey parents (Col. 3:20). Note: If obedience to parents would mean disobeying the word of God—then we must obey God rather than man. There may be many other reasons why we might feel we shouldn't obey, but God has given his word for a good reason, in order that we may benefit. Any resentment or bitterness against parents on our part can cause a barrier between us and God (Heb. 12:14–15). We are not to insult or curse—that is, do not speak ill of or abusively against either parent. Under the Old Testament Law this was punishable by death, and although under the New Covenant this is not the case, it may still result in great spiritual loss.

7:11–13 But you say that if anyone tells his father or mother, 'Whatever help you would have received from me is corban' (that is, a gift for God), then you no longer permit him to do anything for his father or mother. Thus you nullify the word of God by your tradition that you have handed down. And you do many things like this.'

The Pharisees, however, taught that it was pious for a son or daughter to dedicate that financial help which would have been given to their parents to the Temple fund instead. The result of this was that children—adult children—were not caring or providing for their parents in old age, which was in contradiction to God's word (1 Tim. 5:8).

Heart the Centre of Man's Inward Life

7:14 Then he called the crowd again and said to them, 'Listen to me, everyone, and understand.

Having dealt with the Pharisees and scribes Jesus now turns his attention to the crowds for what he is about to say concerned everyone present, just as it concerns everyone today. It is not enough for people just to listen; they need to understand what is being said.

7:15 There is nothing outside of a person that can defile him by going into him. Rather, it is what comes out of a person that defiles him.

(7:16) (TEXT OMITTED)

What he says here in parable form is that it is not the things around us or even the things we say or do outwardly that corrupt us; it is the things that come out of a sinful heart that defile and make us unclean.

7:17–18 Now when Jesus had left the crowd and entered the house, his disciples asked him about the parable. He said to them, 'Are you so foolish? Don't you understand that whatever goes into a person from outside cannot defile him?

Jesus' disciples were still dull and hard of hearing; by now they should have understood what he was saying, but they did not. How patient the Lord is! He rebukes them, but gently. They could not understand the simple truth and so he explained it to them again in such a way that they could not fail to do so.

7:19–20 For it does not enter his heart but his stomach, and then goes out into the sewer.' (This means all foods are clean.) He said, 'What comes out of a person defiles him.

The food that we eat goes into the stomach not into the heart. Then travels through the digestive system where the goodness is extracted and feeds the body, while the poisons or wastes are passed out of the body into the sewer. Hence there is no food that can make us spiritually better or worse off (1 Cor. 8:8).

7:21–23 For from within, out of the human heart, come evil ideas, sexual immorality, theft, murder, adultery, greed, evil, deceit, debauchery, envy, slander, pride, and folly. All these evils come from within and defile a person.

What defiles human nature comes from within the heart (Rom. 7:17) Paul refers to it as the Law of Sin (Rom. 7:23). Jesus makes it quite clear that we sin because we are sinners, not that we are sinners because we sin. He gives a familiar list of the acts of sin that come from a sinful heart and heads it with evil thoughts for that is where they grow until they become acts of sin.

Persistent Asking
7:24 After Jesus left there, he went to the region of Tyre. When he went into a house, he did not want anyone to know, but he was not able to escape notice.

Jesus departs from those to whom he was sent, the Jews, and goes into Syria which was a Gentile country, to the area of Tyre and Sidon. Tyre was a very important seaport and is in fact an island just off the shore. Sidon was about twenty miles away from there. Because this was Gentile country it would seem that Jesus for a while needed a time of rest from the people he was sent to minister to (Matt. 15:24). The end of the verse also suggests this, for he did not want anyone to know that he was there. Even so, this was not possible, for one person at least had heard that Jesus was in the area and she had such a desperate need that made her determined that nothing was going to stop her from taking her petition to the Lord.

7:25–26 Instead, a woman whose young daughter had an unclean spirit immediately heard about him and came and fell at his feet. The woman was a Greek, of Syrophoenician origin. She asked him to cast the demon out of her daughter.

This woman by nationality was a Syrophoenician, that is, she was a Phoenician living in Syria and as such was a Gentile. The point of this incident is to show that the fame of Jesus and news of the miracles he had done crossed national boundaries. This woman having heard all about him sought him out. She did not come to him for her own need but for that of her daughter who was possessed by a demon. Such was the love that this woman had for her daughter that she was prepared to go to whatever lengths necessary to help her. Yet even a mother's love cannot exceed the love of God (Isaiah 49:15).

Although this woman could claim nothing that would commend her to Jesus, and however slim she might have thought the chance of him granting her an audience, she does not hesitate. She falls at his feet in all humility and begs him to deliver her daughter. In Matthew 15:22–23 we are told that she cried to him using his title that only the Jews would use of their Messiah "Lord, Son of David". She had no right to use that name, and indeed, Jesus completely ignored her. When she persisted in spite of this snub, the disciples begged him to send her away. But the woman would not be put off by anything. Was the Lord being completely ignorant and inattentive to this woman's need? Did he have no compassion for her daughter? Was he testing her faith, or affirming that he had come as Messiah to the Jews and not for Gentiles?

7:27 He said to her, 'Let the children be satisfied first, for it is not right to take the children's bread and to throw it to the dogs.'

Matthew's version of this incident would seem to indicate that there was nothing available for non-Jews, for Matthew reports Jesus saying, "It is not right to take the children's bread and throw it to the dogs". Mark's version is somewhat more conciliatory, for Jesus tells her that he has come to the Jew first—that it was their day of opportunity to receive from him all that the Father had given to him, and that it was not right to take that which belonged to the children of Israel and give it to those who had no claims to being in covenant with God (the dogs—the Gentiles).

The Jews were God's chosen people (Deut. 14:2) and he had separated them to himself so that through them the Saviour of the world might come. Mark's rendering of the incident leaves the door open for a later ministry to the Gentiles, but insists that this time had not yet come. God had never planned to exclude Gentiles from obtaining salvation, his Messiah would become a light to all nations (Isaiah 42:6; Luke 2:32). But in the plan of God first the nation of Israel must receive her Messiah, and then through Israel (rather, through a believing remnant within Israel) the message of salvation would be brought to the Gentiles. Indeed, in a way which Paul describes as a mystery, the fact that the majority of Israel did not receive Jesus was part of God's plan, as it led the early church to reach out to the Gentiles (Acts 13:46–47; 14:27; Rom. 11:11).

7:28 She answered, 'Yes, Lord, but even the dogs under the table eat the children's crumbs.'

The woman was not offended or discouraged by Jesus' remark but accepted that what he said was quite true. Even so, she said, the dogs under the table that waited for the crumbs to fall that they might eat them. She accepted that as a Gentile she had no claims to the promises made to the children of Israel, but appealed to the mercy of God to receive whatever overflowed from Israel's blessings.

7:29 Then he said to her, 'Because you said this, you may go. The demon has left your daughter.'

Here it is recorded that for this saying the Lord cast out the demon from her daughter. In Matthew 15:28 it records that Jesus said "Woman, your faith is great! Let what you want be done for you."

7:30 She went home and found the child lying on the bed, and the demon gone.

And when she arrived home she found her daughter delivered just as Jesus had said. This is the only record of Jesus delivering someone from demon possession from a distance. This was also the first definite healing of a Gentile.

The Faith of Faithful Friends

7:31 Then Jesus went out again from the region of Tyre and came through Sidon to the Sea of Galilee in the region of the Decapolis.

Jesus did not prolong his stay in Syria. In the same way that Jesus had to pass through Samaria (John 4:4) to meet a woman in the town of Sychar, perhaps he also needed to go to Syria to deliver this woman's daughter.

7:32 They brought to him a deaf man who had difficulty speaking, and they asked him to place his hands on him.

The friends of the deaf and dumb man proved to be friends indeed, those who could be trusted and depended on (Prov. 17:17; 18:24). It is in their faithfulness to him that they bring him to Jesus and it is their faith in Jesus that brings the man his healing.

7:33 After Jesus took him aside privately, away from the crowd, he put his fingers in the man's ears, and after spitting, he touched his tongue.

The Lord handles this man in a special way, as he always does—as an individual. He considered the man's condition, being deaf he would not be able to hear what Jesus said to him, hence the Lord uses a type of sign language so that the man could understand what he was going to do. He puts his fingers in his ears, to show that he was going to heal his deafness, the touch of the tongue to enable him to speak.

7:34–35 Then he looked up to heaven and said with a sigh, 'Ephphatha' (that is, 'Be opened'). And immediately the man's ears were opened, his tongue loosened, and he spoke plainly.

Jesus' looking up to heaven would tell the man that Jesus was praying for him. At the command "Ephphatha, be opened" he immediately heard and was able to speak without any impediment, a complete healing.

7:36 Jesus ordered them not to tell anything. But as much as he ordered them not to do this, they proclaimed it all the more.

Again Jesus commanded the people not to say anything about what had happened; but once again they disobeyed and published it all the more.

7:37 People were completely astounded and said, 'He has done everything well. He even makes the deaf hear and the mute speak.'

This time the people were overwhelmed with amazement that Jesus was able to make the deaf to hear and the dumb to speak and declare that he had done everything excellently. This remark echoes the words in Genesis 1 after every act of creation "God saw all that he had made and behold it was very good."

Discussion Questions for Chapter 7

1. vv. 1–16. Why do you think that outward religious rituals such as washing can never take away sins?

2. Read Revelation 1:5. What can wash away our sins?

3. vv. 6–13. In what way did Jesus say the Pharisees had disregarded the commandments of God?

4. vv. 14–23. Explain in your own words why nothing entering a person's body can make that person unclean in God's sight.

5. vv. 24–30. What lessons can we learn about prayer from the Syrophoenician woman?

You will find suggested answers to the study questions on pages 183–193.

Mark Chapter 8

The Lord Provides

This feeding of the four thousand is not a repeat account of the feeding of the five thousand. It is a separate miracle and there are a few differences in it. It is these differences that we will note.

8:1–4 In those days there was another large crowd with nothing to eat. So Jesus called his disciples and said to them, "I have compassion on the crowd, because they have already been here with me three days, and they have nothing to eat. If I send them home hungry, they will faint on the way, and some of them have come from a great distance." His disciples answered him, "Where can someone get enough bread in this desolate place to satisfy these people?"

These people had hungered and thirsted for the "bread of heaven"—God's word—for three days and had received this from the mouth of Jesus. Now Jesus could see that they were physically in need of nourishment and would not have enough strength to go to the towns to get food. Moved with compassion, he does not on this occasion challenge the faith of the disciples by directly asking them to feed the people; instead he simply states his concern for the people.

8:5–6 He asked them, "How many loaves do you have?" They replied, "Seven." Then he directed the crowd to sit down on the ground. After he took the seven loaves and gave thanks, he broke them and began giving them to the disciples to serve. So they served the crowd.

Since the disciples were not forthcoming with a suggestion that he should repeat his earlier miracle, Jesus asked how many loaves they had brought with them. This should have reminded them of the earlier incident. Then he directed the crowd to sit down on the ground, took the seven loaves and gave thanks, broke them and gave them out to the disciples so that they might serve the people.

8:7–9 They also had a few small fish. After giving thanks for these, he told them to serve these as well. Everyone ate and was satisfied, and they picked up the broken pieces left over, seven baskets full. There were about four thousand who ate. Then he dismissed them.

This time it is seven loaves and a few fish, which he also blessed and instructed his disciples to give out among the people. So they all ate sufficiently and this time there were seven baskets left over. Seven in the scriptures is a perfect number. The Lord had perfectly provided just what the people needed, and he still does. Do we give thanks in everything and for everything even the small things? Do we bless God for the little things as well as the great things that he gives to us?

Sign Seekers

8:11 Then the Pharisees came and began to argue with Jesus, asking for a sign from heaven to test him.

The Pharisees approached Jesus with no other thought in their minds but to dispute with him concerning his teaching and his claims to be God's son. They demand a sign as proof that he was what he claimed to be. This was a malicious test; they did not really want to see a sign and even if they did they still would not have believed. People are the same today; many say that they would believe if they saw a miracle, but this is just an excuse for not believing.

8:12 Sighing deeply in his spirit he said, 'Why does this generation look for a sign? I tell you the truth; no sign will be given to this generation.'

In response, Jesus groaned in his spirit, being greatly disturbed by their unbelief, and challenged their lack of faith. No sign would be given to those who stubbornly refused to obey, but (as in Matthew 16:4) only the sign of Jonah. For as Jonah was in the whale's belly for three days and nights so Jesus would be in the tomb three days and nights and then rise from the dead.

In the story of Lazarus and the rich man Abraham said "If they hear not Moses and the prophets, neither will they be persuaded though one rose from the dead (Luke 16:27–31). The Pharisees and many other people had it the wrong way round; faith must be present *before* God works miracles. In Mark 16:17 Jesus said "these signs shall follow them *that believe*" and verse 20 "they went forth, and preached everywhere, the Lord working with them, and confirming the word with signs following".

Warning against Corrupt Teaching

8:13–14 Then he left them, got back into the boat, and went to the other side. Now they had forgotten to take bread, except for one loaf they had with them in the boat.

Once again Jesus and the disciples are in the boat and this time the disciples were in a dilemma because they had forgotten to get bread and were conscious of the fact that they only had one loaf between them.

8:15 And Jesus ordered them, 'Watch out! Beware of the yeast of the Pharisees and the yeast of Herod!'

This was the uppermost thought in their minds when Jesus turned and warned them to be on their guard against the leaven of the Pharisees, of Herod and in Matthew's gospel the Sadducees as well. Leaven is sour dough that is highly fermented and used for making bread rise. In the New Testament the word is used to mean corruption because the sour dough placed in the bread contaminates, as it were, the whole loaf (see 1 Cor. 5:7).

8:16 So they began to discuss with one another about having no bread.

But the disciples were so earthly minded that they thought he was rebuking them for not bringing enough bread.

8:17–21 When he learned of this, Jesus said to them, 'Why are you arguing about having no bread? Do you still not see or understand? Have your hearts been hardened? Though you have eyes, don't you see? And though you have ears, can't you hear? Don't you remember? When I broke the five loaves for the five thousand, how many baskets full of pieces did you pick up?' They replied, 'Twelve.' 'When I broke the seven loaves for the four thousand, how many baskets full of pieces did you pick up?' They replied, 'Seven.' Then he said to them, 'Do you still not understand?'

Jesus rebukes them for having no understanding; they had been with him long enough to know better but had hardened their hearts in unbelief. He rebuked them for being spiritually blind even after he had opened their eyes to the truth and for their spiritual deafness because what he had taught them had evidently not sunk in. He further rebuked them for not remembering what he had done in providing for the five thousand and four thousand. So why were they bothering about not having enough food when they had seen him provide in this way? And why did they not understand the spiritual lessons he had taught them by it?

In Matthew 16:11–12 it says he then told them plainly that he wasn't talking about bread to eat but that he was warning them to be on guard against corrupt teaching (see Col. 2:8; Heb. 13:9). The warning still holds for today; the devil still comes as an angel of light seeking to deceive. Corrupt teaching is *based* on the truth but has been altered to suit the doctrines of men and wicked angels.

Opening Blind Eyes

8:22 Then they came to Bethsaida. They brought a blind man to Jesus and asked him to touch him.

After rebuking his disciples for their spiritual blindness, Jesus arrives at Bethsaida where a blind man is brought by his friends to be healed.

8:23 He took the blind man by the hand and brought him outside of the village. Then he spit on his eyes, placed his hands on his eyes and asked, 'Do you see anything?'

He takes the man from the hustle and bustle of the town to a quiet place where he spits on his eyes. Was this another sign language to show the man that he was going to open his eyes? There doesn't seem to be any other reason why he should do this for it was his touch upon the man that would bring the healing.

8:24–26 Regaining his sight he said, 'I see people, but they look like trees walking.' Then Jesus placed his hands on the man's eyes again. And he opened his eyes, his sight was restored, and he saw everything clearly. Jesus sent him home, saying, 'Do not even go into the village.'

This is the only healing recorded that was not complete first time, for the man saw figures walking about but not clearly. Jesus laid his hands on the man again until he received perfect sight. It could not have been any lack on the Lord's part as to why this man did not receive his sight straight away. It has been suggested that perhaps the Lord saw a lack of faith in the man that caused this. In Matthew 9:29 Jesus said "according to your faith let it be to you". In order to keep the miracle quiet, Jesus told the man to go home immediately, and not into the village.

Revelation Given by God—Peter gets it Right

8:27–28 Then Jesus and his disciples went to the villages of Caesarea Philippi. On the way he asked his disciples, 'Who do people say that I am?' They said, 'John the Baptist, others say Elijah, and still others, one of the prophets.'

So far the disciples had not been doing so well, but they were still in the preparation stage and the day of Pentecost has not yet arrived when the Holy Spirit would be given (John 16:13–14). In these verses Jesus tested them to see if they had fully realised who he really was. First of all he asked "who do the people say I am". They replied either John the Baptist, risen from the dead, because of the way he preached, or Elijah, who had not died but was taken to heaven in a fiery chariot (2 Kings 2:11), this was because of the miracles that he did, and since many believed that Elijah would come back to prepare the way for the Messiah. It was in fact John the Baptist who fulfilled this role (Matt. 11:14).

8:29–30 He asked them, 'But who do you say that I am?' Peter answered him, 'You are the Christ.' Then he warned them not to tell anyone about him.

He then asked the disciples "who do you say I am" and it was Peter who confessed that he is "the Christ". Peter did not arrive at this conclusion because of his own knowledge or ability to understand. Neither did he receive it from other men, but Jesus said that the Father had revealed it to him (Matt. 16:17). Yet even though Peter confessed Jesus as the Christ by the revelation that God gave him, he did not fully understand the implications of this, as the next verses show.

Deception Given by Satan—Peter gets it Wrong

8:31 Then Jesus began to teach them that the Son of Man must suffer many things and be rejected by the elders, chief priests, and experts in the law, and be killed, and after three days rise again.

For the first time Jesus tells his disciples in plain terms that the purpose he came into the world was to suffer and die, but that he would rise again after three days.

8:32 He spoke openly about this. So Peter took him aside and began to rebuke him.

He spoke about this publicly, so that many would hear and know. To Peter, this seemed as if the Lord was being defeatist and did not know what he was talking about. Had not he only just commenced his ministry? Weren't the people gladly hearing and accepting him? Didn't Jesus have many years of fruitful ministry before him? To talk of dying was ludicrous! But this time Peter got it all wrong and took it upon himself to rebuke the Lord for saying such things. Peter made the mistake of looking at things through his own eyes and with his own level of understanding (see the wise advice of Prov. 3:5), and by so doing he gave Satan an opportunity of sneaking up to use him.

8:33 But after turning and looking at his disciples, he rebuked Peter and said, 'Get behind me, Satan. You are not setting your mind on God's interests, but on man's.'

Jesus was concerned about the effect Peter's statement would have on the faith of his disciples. Peter's action was in complete contradiction to what the Lord had said. It was an attempt by Satan to use a human agent to obstruct Jesus from doing his Father's will. Jesus therefore commands the Devil to get behind him (James 4:7) and rebukes Peter for giving in to Satan by seeing things only with an earthly mind. Peter had his mind fixed on an earthly kingdom instead of a heavenly. We are to set our minds on things above not on things on the earth (Col. 3:2). Let us make certain we do not make the same mistake as Peter.

True Discipleship
8:34 Then Jesus called the crowd, along with his disciples, and said to them, 'If anyone wants to become my follower, he must deny himself, take up his cross, and follow me.

The qualifications that the Lord requires for all who desire to become his disciples are the same for all time. Here he calls all the people to him that they may clearly understand what it would mean to follow him. "Whoever will come after", that is, whoever decides to join or identify himself with me, must "deny himself"—forget, disown, lose sight of himself and his own interests, not seeking to please himself but to do God's will. The Lord desires that we should be in the relationship with him that Paul was when he said "I count everything as loss compared with the possession of the priceless privilege of knowing Jesus Christ my Lord, and of progressively becoming more deeply and intimately acquainted with him...for his sake I have lost everything and consider it to be mere rubbish, in order that I may be the possession of Christ." (Phil. 3:8 Amp. N. T.)

If we would be wholly Christ's then we will have to give up all claims on ourselves. This means that we must willingly say that we are no longer our own, but have been bought with a great price. We must renounce all claims on ourselves and give our all into the hands of Christ Jesus. "Take up his cross" (the original word meant "stake")—the people of Christ's day would have been familiar with the sight of criminals carrying the crosses they would be crucified on. To the disciples the full meaning of Christ's words would not be fully understood until after he had borne his cross to be crucified.

So was Jesus saying to them, and to us, that we must bear a cross and be crucified? I believe that he is saying three things here that just as it was the Father's purpose for Jesus to come into the world and give his life for us, suffering the shame and reproach of the cross, so as his disciples we too must give our lives in sacrificial service to him, and be willing to do whatever he asks of us no matter what the cost. Firstly, we must put off of the flesh with its passions and lusts (Eph. 4:22), spiritually identifying ourselves with Christ in his death (Rom. 6:6). "Follow me"—in the children's game of "follow the leader" you have to copy everything the leader does and so what Jesus was saying here is that we are to follow the example and standard of his life (1 Pet. 2:21).

8:35 For whoever wants to save his life will lose it, but whoever loses his life for my sake and for the gospel will save it.

The life that Jesus refers to here in the first part is spiritual life. If anyone wants to save his (spiritual) life then he has to deny the lower nature, the temporal life which is lived on the earth (1 John 2:15–16).

Whoever gives up control of his life for the Lord's sake and the Gospel's will have eternal life (Gal. 2:20).

8:36 For what benefit is it for a person to gain the whole world, yet forfeit his life?

In asking this question the Lord challenges his hearers to examine their values. What do they consider to be the most important thing in life? What good is it for a man or woman to have all that this world can offer and yet at the end of it lose their own soul? Like the farmer who built bigger barns to store his crops and thought that he would live to enjoy them, giving no thought for eternal things, neglecting his soul, they are fools. For in the case of that farmer, Jesus said that his life was taken from him that night and all the wealth he had accumulated left to someone else (Luke 12:16–21).

8:37 What can a person give in exchange for his life?

What price can a person pay for their own soul in return for a blessed life in the kingdom of God? Of course the answer is that people are so spiritually bankrupt that they cannot pay the price. It was Jesus Christ, God's own Son, that paid the ransom price for our souls (1 Pet. 1:18–19).

8:38 For if anyone is ashamed of me and my words in this adulterous and sinful generation, the Son of Man will also be ashamed of him when he comes in the glory of his Father with the holy angels.'

Jesus warned those who accepted the words he spoke to never be ashamed to own him or have a fear that might prevent them from keeping faithful to his words before an unfaithful and sinful people (the unsaved). He says that in the day when he returns (2 Cor. 5:10) he will also disown such people (Luke 12:9).

Discussion Questions for Chapter 8

1. vv. 1–9. What do you think is significant about Jesus repeating his earlier miracle of feeding a great crowd of people?

2. vv. 11–12. Why do you think the Pharisees demanded signs from Jesus?

3. vv. 13–21. In what ways is false teaching like yeast?

4. vv. 22–26. Can you think of any reason why the blind man's healing occurred in two stages?

5. vv. 34–38. In your own words describe what it costs to truly follow Jesus Christ.

You will find suggested answers to the study questions on pages 183–193.

Mark Chapter 9

The Glory of the Coming Kingdom

9:1 And he said to them, 'I tell you the truth, there are some standing here who will not experience death before they see the kingdom of God come with power.'

What did Jesus mean? There were those who were standing among the people who would still be alive when the kingdom of God was ushered in; that is, after the death and resurrection of the Lord Jesus Christ. From that time on the kingdom would be seen amongst the people, coming into being with great power (probably a reference to Pentecost).

9:2–3 Six days later Jesus took with him Peter, James, and John and led them alone up a high mountain privately. And he was transfigured before them, and his clothes became radiantly white, more so than any launderer in the world could bleach them.

Jesus chose Peter, James and John to go with him to the summit of a high mountain where they could be alone. Jesus' choice of these three was not based on favouritism, for we are all equal in God's sight (Acts 10:34). Rather, it appears that these three were the most spiritually responsive to the teachings of Christ.

Whilst they were on the mountain (presumably in prayer) Jesus' physical body was transformed as the glory which he had with the Father before he came to earth shone through (John 17:5). The disciples saw his eternal glory shining from him to such an extent that his garments appeared whiter than anything on earth.

9:4 Then Elijah appeared before them along with Moses, and they were talking with Jesus.

The text does not explicitly state that the disciples recognised Elijah and Moses; the Lord may have addressed them by name. The presence of these two men was full of significance. For Elijah represented the prophets, and Moses the law of God. Jesus Christ is the fulfilment of both the law and the prophets.

One would very much like to know what they were talking about with Jesus. It seems most likely that it was concerned with his approaching crucifixion and the salvation that he would obtain through it. These two men had waited in faith for this salvation; and the sacrifice of Christ which made our salvation possible is the endless theme of the glorified saints in heaven (Rev. 5:9).

9:5–6 So Peter said to Jesus, 'Rabbi, it is good for us to be here. Let us make three shelters—one for you, one for Moses, and one for Elijah.' (For they were afraid, and he did not know what to say.)

The disciples seemingly could not understand what was happening, and this strangeness brought fear to their hearts. Peter, for want of something to say, proposed to build three booths (made of tree branches) for each of them. Such booths were often made as temporary protection from the hot sun. The text does not reveal what Peter had in mind—for he did not know himself! Even so, Peter did get one thing right—it was good for them to be there. What better place could there be than where we can behold the beauty and the glory of the Lord?

9:7 Then a cloud overshadowed them, and a voice came from the cloud, 'This is my one dear Son. Listen to him!'

At this point God intervened, descending in a cloud which covered the frightened disciples. As he spoke to them, acknowledging Jesus as his beloved Son, God gave these disciples the true lesson which the experience was meant to teach them—by commanding that they should listen to and obey Jesus.

9:8 Suddenly when they looked around, they saw no one with them any more except Jesus.

Suddenly it was all over—the cloud, the voice, Elijah and Moses had gone; only Jesus remained.

9:9 As they were coming down from the mountain, he gave them orders not to tell anyone what they had seen until after the Son of Man had risen from the dead.

As they were coming back down the mountain Jesus strictly ordered them to tell no one about the things they had seen until after he had risen from the dead.

9:10 They kept this statement to themselves, discussing what this rising from the dead meant.

And this is what they did; although they did not understand what he meant about being raised from the dead.

9:9–13 Then they asked him, 'Why do the experts in the law say that Elijah must come first?' He said to them, 'Elijah does indeed come first, and restores all things. And why is it written that the Son of Man must suffer many things and be despised? But I tell you that Elijah has certainly come, and they did to him whatever they wanted, just as it is written about him.'

Realising afresh from this experience that Jesus was the Christ, the Son of God, the disciples asked why the experts in the law taught that Elijah (whom they had witnessed speaking with Jesus) must first come before the Christ would be manifested (Mal. 4:5–6). Jesus replied that the lawyers were correct in their interpretation of scripture, for truly someone must first come in the spirit and power of Elijah to make Israel ready to receive the Christ. But this Elijah-type role had been fulfilled by John the Baptist (Luke 1:17); and just as the religious and political leaders of Israel had rejected John and mistreated him, so they were about to do to Jesus.

Belief and Unbelief

9:14 When they came to the disciples, they saw a large crowd around them and experts in the law arguing with them.

While the three disciples were with Jesus enjoying the mountain top experience the other nine were having a tough time down in the valley. When Jesus returned, he found these disciples being interrogated by the scribes and losing the argument.

9:15 When the whole crowd saw him, they were amazed and ran at once and greeted him.

Something of the glory of the transfiguration must have still been upon the Lord, for when the people saw him they were amazed at his appearance and eagerly ran to greet and welcome him.

9:16 He asked them, 'What are you arguing about with them?'

Seeing his disciples greatly disturbed, he asked them what they were discussing. This was not because Jesus did not know, but he wanted to bring the subject out into open discussion.

9:17 A member of the crowd said to him, 'Teacher, I brought you my son, who is possessed by a spirit that makes him mute.

Neither the scribes nor the disciples answered him; instead someone from among the crowd called out. He had brought his son who was possessed by a dumb spirit to Jesus to be delivered.

9:18 Whenever it seizes him, it throws him down, and he foams at the mouth, grinds his teeth, and becomes rigid. I asked your disciples to cast it out, but they were not able to do so.

On discovering that Jesus was not with the disciples, he had turned to them expecting that they could cast out the dumb spirit. The man must have heard of, or perhaps had witnessed, the disciples casting out demons when Jesus sent them on an earlier mission (Mark 6:13). By the description that the man gave it would seem that it was only at certain times that this demon took hold of his son, throwing him into a fit which left him almost lifeless, and that it was slowly destroying his body. The disciples had been powerless to cast out this demon.

9:19–20 He answered them, 'You unbelieving generation! How much longer must I be with you? How much longer must I endure you? Bring him to me.' So they brought the boy to him. When the spirit saw him, it immediately threw the boy into a convulsion. He fell on the ground and rolled around, foaming at the mouth.

One might wonder to whom the Lord addressed these words: the scribes, the crowd, the father of the boy or to his own disciples. They are certainly words of rebuke to all who have no faith. They would certainly apply to the scribes, who did not believe in Jesus at all. There were probably many in the crowd who were sceptical of Jesus' claims. The father of the boy had some faith in bringing his son to Jesus in the first place, yet confesses later that his faith is small. What about the disciples? The Lord had rebuked them on a previous occasions for lacking faith (Mark 4:40). So perhaps all of those standing there merited the rebuke.

Jesus reproof was aimed at provoking faith in those who lacked it. When he asked "how long must I endure you?" he already knew the answer; for he knew when his hour would come. As the boy was brought to Jesus the demon immediately manifested itself in the presence of the authority and power of Christ, throwing the boy to the ground in a convulsion.

9:21–22 Jesus asked his father, 'How long has this been happening to him?' And he said, 'From childhood. It has often thrown him into fire or water to destroy him. But if you are able to do anything, have compassion on us and help us.'

Jesus' purpose in asking the boy's father for details of his son's condition was not to enable a diagnosis, but to bring a full realization to the father and the disciples of the hold and length of time the demon had bound this child (the importance of this fact is brought out later in verse 29).

9:23 Then Jesus said to him, 'If you are able? All things are possible for the one who believes.'

Jesus placed the responsibility for the boy's deliverance on the father. "If you can believe—for all things are possible to him that believes." This is a promise that we can also claim (see Mark 11:24).

9:24 Immediately the father of the boy cried out and said, 'I believe; help my unbelief!'

The man realized what Jesus was saying to him and knowing his own deficiency gave out a heart rending cry; and, weeping, confessed "Lord, I believe" but, "constantly help my weakness in faith" (Amp. N. T.) or "when I begin to doubt help me to continue to believe".

9:25 Now when Jesus saw that a crowd was quickly gathering, he rebuked the unclean spirit, saying to it, 'Mute and deaf spirit, I command you, come out of him and never enter him again.'

On seeing the crowds approaching, the Lord immediately rebuked the unclean spirit and commanded it to come out of the boy. He further charged the spirit never to enter him again (this is the only time that it is recorded that Jesus said this).

9:26 It shrieked, threw him into terrible convulsions, and came out. The boy looked so much like a corpse that many said, 'He is dead!'

The demon did not leave willingly; yet it simply had no choice but to obey the authority of Jesus. Such was the violent exit of the demon that the boy appeared to be dead.

9:27 But Jesus gently took his hand and raised him to his feet, and he stood up.

But whenever the Lord delivers or heals he does so completely without any adverse effects. Taking the boy by the hand, Jesus lifted him; he had been made completely whole.

9:28 Then, after he went into the house, his disciples asked him privately, 'Why couldn't we cast it out?'

The disciples were eager to find out why it was that they had failed to deliver the boy. Was it their lack of faith? It is always good for us to enquire of the Lord why we seem to fail at something which we have tried to do for him.

9:29 He told them, 'This kind can come out only by prayer.'

Jesus tells them that it was not their lack of faith alone which hindered them. The demon was so powerful and had such a hold on the boy (having possessed him since he was a young child) that it could only be effectively dealt with after time spent in prayer and fasting.

A Quiet Time with Jesus

9:30 They went out from there and passed through Galilee. But Jesus did not want anyone to know,

At last Jesus found an opportunity to spend time with his disciples alone, leading them through Galilee in order to avoid the crowds. There are times when the Lord leads us in quiet paths so that he might teach us and show us the way in which he would guide us.

9:31–32 for he was teaching his disciples and telling them, 'The Son of Man will be betrayed into the hands of men. They will kill him, and after three days he will rise.' But they did not understand this statement and were afraid to ask him.

Jesus wanted to use this time to teach his disciples. Mark records only a summary of the content of Christ's teaching: the Son of Man (Jesus may have explained to them the meaning of his preferred title—that it meant him to be God manifest in human form) would be delivered into the hands of men and killed; and that he would be raised from the dead on the third day. Whether or not Jesus went into greater details about his offering of himself being sacrifice for sin, or about his resurrection bringing victory over death is not clear. Whatever the case, the disciples clearly did not understand what he was saying to them and were afraid to ask him to explain it more clearly.

The Greatest is the Least

9:33 Then they came to Capernaum. After Jesus was inside the house he asked them, 'What were you discussing on the way?'

On their way to Capernaum all was not well between the disciples; for a dispute had arisen among them (which they thought the Lord had not heard) about which of them was to be the greatest. Jesus, as the Master, would have walked in front and the disciples would have followed in single file behind him; so it was quite possible for them to talk among themselves without Jesus hearing. Nevertheless, when they arrived at the house they were surprised and embarrassed when Jesus asked them what they had been arguing about. He knew of course; for nothing is hid from his sight or hearing (Heb. 4:12–13).

9:34 But they were silent, for on the way they had argued with one another about who was the greatest.

The disciples were too ashamed to admit that they had been arguing about who would be the most important and have the most honoured place in the kingdom of God. They were all rather ambitious and sought to exalt themselves.

9:35 After he sat down, he called the twelve and said to them, 'If anyone wants to be first, he must be last of all and servant of all.'

Jesus soon brought them down to earth as he sat with them to resolve the argument. Whoever has a desire to be first, or the greatest, must humble himself and consider himself to be the least and servant of all.

9:36 He took a little child and had him stand among them. Taking him in his arms, he said to them,

Taking a little child, Jesus placed him in the middle of the disciples so that they might compare their self-importance with the boy's humility. Then he takes the child into his arms to show that those who become as little children are the ones welcomed in the kingdom of heaven (Matt. 18:4).

9:37 'Whoever welcomes one of these little children in my name welcomes me, and whoever welcomes me does not welcome me but the one who sent me.'

Whoever accepts and receives a child in the Lord's name, and for his sake, is counted as having received Jesus Christ and the Father who sent him into the world to save sinners (1 Tim. 1:15).

In My Name

9:38–40 John said to him, 'Teacher, we saw someone casting out demons in your name, and we tried to stop him because he was not following us.' But Jesus said, 'Do not stop him, because no one who does a miracle in my name will be able soon afterward to say anything bad about me. For whoever is not against us is for us

Jesus gave the nickname "sons of thunder" to James and John because of their quick tempers (Mark 3:17). On one occasion they wanted to call down fire from heaven to destroy a Samaritan village where they were unwelcome (Luke 9:54). In this section John complains to Jesus about someone, who was not among the disciples, using Jesus' name to cast out demons. John (and presumably James) became very indignant about this and forbade the man to use the name of Jesus because he was not a disciple. It is quite possible that their reaction arose from their own self-importance rather than any concern about Jesus' reputation. They thought they had exclusive rights to use the name of the Lord, and had perhaps forgotten that it was Jesus by his grace who had given them permission to use his name. The point is that only Jesus can grant or deny permission to use his name, and he has given all believers the right to use his name in prayer (John 14:13). Through his name we have life (John 20:31) and in that name even the weakest believer may cast out demons and heal the sick (Mark 16:17–18).

Jesus corrects the disciples' exclusivism; for no one who does a mighty work in his name would soon afterwards speak evil of him. What the man was doing would only serve to advance the interests of the gospel and therefore the disciples. Either a person is for Jesus or against him, for no one can be indifferent as far as Christ is concerned (Luke 11:23).

9:41 For I tell you the truth, whoever gives you a cup of water because you bear Christ's name will never lose his reward.

If anyone gives even a cup of water to those who belong to Christ and bear his name, they will not fail to receive a reward.

Causing Offence

9:42 'If anyone causes one of these little ones who believe in me to sin, it would be better for him to have a huge millstone tied around his neck and to be thrown into the sea.

The child whom Jesus took into his arms in verse 36 must have still been there for Jesus again uses him to illustrate this point about offences. Yet what Jesus says does not only refer to little children but to all who believe in him as Saviour and Lord.

Jesus said "except you are be converted, and become like little children, you shall not enter the kingdom of heaven" (Matt. 18:3). Throughout the New Testament believers are referred to as "children" or "little children". The warning Jesus gave is that if anyone caused those who belong to him to stumble into sin then it would be better for them if they were tied to a millstone and drowned in the sea. We should be careful not to do anything that could cause a brother or sister to fall (Rom. 14:13). John says that if we love one another and abide in the light then we will not give an occasion to cause anyone to stumble and turn away from Christ (1 John 2:10).

Cutting off the Source of Temptation

9:43–48 If your hand causes you to sin, cut it off! It is better for you to enter into life crippled than to have two hands and go into hell, to the unquenchable fire. If your foot causes you to sin, cut it off! It is better to enter life lame than to have two feet and be thrown into hell. If your eye causes you to sin, tear it out! It is better to enter into the kingdom of God with one eye than to have two eyes and be thrown into hell, where their worm never dies and the fire is never quenched.

In some countries offenders who break the law of the land are punished by various amputations. For example, a hand may be cut off a convicted thief. It is clear, however, that the disciples understood that when Jesus spoke of "cutting off" body parts that his words were not meant to be taken literally—for they neither practised nor preached mutilation.

Whatever "causes you to sin" is to be "cut off". The scripture teaches us to mortify or account as dead the parts of our body so far as their being used for sinful purposes is concerned. In Romans 6:6 Paul puts it this way: "our old self was nailed to the cross with him (Christ) in order that our body which is the instrument of sin, might be made ineffective, and inactive for evil, that we may no longer be the slaves of sin" (Amp. N. T.). When we face many temptations which are hard to resist, Paul exhorts, "walk in the Spirit, and you shall not fulfil the lusts of the flesh" (Gal. 5:16). So it is not by cutting off parts of our body that we can overcome sin, but by refusing to live according to the old ways, and live instead according to a new life principle—that if the Spirit of life.

Although it may appear that by taking such action to resist sin we are losing out in life, the reverse is actually true, for we can only gain by living out the abundant life that Christ has given to us. Of this Christ-life, Paul wrote, "for me to live is Christ, and to die is gain" (Phil. 1:21). There is only one alternative to eternal life and that is the second death (hell or Gehenna) where those who have not received Jesus Christ as their Saviour shall go because they choose to live a life of sin rather than live for Christ. The phrase "unquenchable fire" indicates that neither the first death nor the second death mean annihilation; the penalty for sin will go on forever (Rev. 14:11).

By considering the parts of the anatomy which Jesus uses to illustrate his point, we recognise some of the many ways in which temptation allures us. With our hands we take, hold onto or do things. The temptation to steal, covet or do evil must be resisted. As must the temptation to go to places where we should not go or walk in a way displeasing to God (foot). With our eyes we see; they are the gateway to the mind, and so what we see and think upon should be pleasing to God (Phil. 4:8). Since our eyes, feet and hands belong to Christ, we should choose to use them for him alone.

Salt and Fire

9:49 Everyone will be salted with fire.

Everyone's work will be tested by fire to see if what they have done has been carried out with pure and unselfish motives, building on the work that Jesus Christ has done in our lives. All other works will be destroyed (1 Cor. 3:15).

9:50 Salt is good, but if it loses its saltiness, how can you make it salty again? Have salt in yourselves, and be at peace with each other.'

Salt is good for cleansing, purifying and preserving and is essential for the benefit of the body. So the children of God should be a good influence, a good example in the world, and be at peace among ourselves (1 Thess. 5:13)—for if we cannot be at peace, who can be?

Discussion Questions for Chapter 9

1. vv. 15–29. Here was an occasion when the apostles were asked to deliver a boy who was possessed with an evil spirit, but they could not. What lessons might they have learned from this experience?

2. v. 33–37. James and John wanted to be the greatest—but who did Jesus say would be the greatest in the kingdom of God?

3. vv. 38–41. Why do you think John wanted to stop a man doing miracles in Jesus name?

4. vv. 38–41. Why did Jesus tell John not to do this?

5. vv. 42–50. What attitude did Jesus want his followers to have toward sin?

You will find suggested answers to the study questions on pages 183–193.

Mark Chapter 10

Marriage and Divorce

10:1 Then Jesus left that place and went to the region of Judea and beyond the Jordan River. Again crowds gathered to him, and again, as was his custom, he taught them.

The Lord had by now completed his ministry in Galilee and moved into Judea in preparation for his entry into Jerusalem and eventual death. Just as he did in Galilee, he taught the crowds of people who gathered to him.

10:2 Then some Pharisees came, and to test him they asked 'Is it lawful for a man to divorce his wife?'

A group of Pharisees approached Jesus with a question about the legality of divorce. These experts in the Law of Moses were trying to trap Jesus with a difficult question rather than genuinely seeking an answer. They hoped that Jesus might show a lack of moral values and compromise on Biblical ethics.

Sometimes believers are faced with similar testing questions from sceptics. Like the Pharisees these people are not genuinely seeking for answers; they want to make Christians look foolish. Our answers to such questions should always be taken from the word of God and if we are not sure of an answer it is best to admit this rather than make an unsuccessful attempt and so appear foolish.

10:3 He answered them, 'What did Moses command you?'

Jesus threw the ball straight back into their court by asking them what Moses had written concerning divorce.

10:4 They said, 'Moses permitted a man to write a certificate of dismissal and to divorce her.'

Note the wording "Moses permitted"—which suggests that Moses was making a concession for a particular reason when he allowed a man to make out a certificate of divorce and send his wife away (Deut. 24:1).

10:5 But Jesus said to them, 'He wrote this commandment for you because of your hard hearts.

Jesus explained that the reason why this concession became necessary was the perverseness and hardness of heart of the people towards the things of God.

10:6–7 But from the beginning of creation he made them male and female. For this reason a man will leave his father and mother,

Long before the law was given it was the plan and purpose of God to create humankind male and female (Gen. 1:27; Gen. 5:2). God ordained that a man should leave his parents and take a wife; being united to her in marriage (Gen. 2:24) for the rest of their lives (Rom. 7:2). The marriage ends at death, for there is no marriage in heaven (Matt. 22:30); except the "marriage" of the Lamb (Jesus) to his people (Rev. 19:7).

10:8 and the two will become one flesh. So they are no longer two, but one flesh.

By coming together the husband and wife cease to be separate people in the eyes of God; they become one flesh. This does not mean that they are no longer individuals or that one or other's personality disappears, it means that they become regarded as one—a family unit—in God's eyes.

10:9 Therefore what God has joined together, let no one separate.'

Marriage is a sacred institution ordained by God; therefore the solemn charge that Jesus gives is also the answer to the Pharisees question in verse 2. When God has united two together, let no one separate or divide them. The seriousness of the wording here suggests that if anyone should try to separate them then they will fall into the hands of the living God and be punished according to his justice.

10:10 In the house once again, the disciples asked him about this.

This teaching of the Lord's disturbed the disciples. It was quite possible that most of them were married; certainly Peter was (Mark 1:30). They had been brought up to believe that if they wanted to they could dispose of their wives. Perhaps they felt that the words of Jesus were a threat to a privilege they thought they were entitled to. Like the Pharisees they could not see beyond the letter of the law to the Spirit of the law (Rom. 7:6). So when they were with Jesus they asked him to explain the matter further.

10:11–12 So he told them, 'Whoever divorces his wife and marries another commits adultery against her. And if she divorces her husband and marries another, she commits adultery.'

The law said "you shall not commit adultery" (Ex. 20:14), but Jesus added to this "whoever so much as looks at another woman with evil desires for her has already committed adultery" (Matt. 5:28). Here he says that if a man divorces his wife and marries someone else then this is adultery against his first wife (the same applies vice-versa, if the wife divorces her husband and remarries). In Matthew's account of this it records that Jesus said that the only legitimate reason for divorce is fornication (Matt. 19:9). God considers marriage to be so sacred that in Ephesians 5:24–33 the relationship between Christ and his church is likened to a marriage.

Children Important to Jesus

Turning from the subject of marriage and divorce, Jesus next deals with one of the results and purposes of marriage: children (Gen. 1:28). The other main purpose being fellowship according to Genesis 2:18.

10:13 Now people were bringing little children to him for him to touch, but the disciples scolded those who brought them.

Why did the disciples become so angry when the people brought their children to Jesus? They would have been well acquainted with Old Testament which describes God's view of children in these words: "children are a heritage of the Lord" (Ps. 127:3); and they were allowed to be present at religious gatherings (2 Chr. 20:13).

In the New Testament, Jesus reveals that God has set angels to watch over the children (Matt. 18:10) and their praise to the Lord was received by him (Matt. 21:15). Whatever reasons the disciples had for sending the children away their parents knew why they had brought them: that Jesus might touch them and bring the blessing of God onto their lives.

10:14 But when Jesus saw this, he was indignant and said to them, 'Let the little children come to me and do not try to stop them, for the kingdom of God belongs to such as these.

Jesus saw the attitude of his disciples and was angered by their treatment of the children. He commands the disciples to allow the children to come to him, and explains that even little children may believe and so enter the kingdom of heaven. Indeed, recent surveys suggest that the majority of people who become Christians do so before their fifteenth birthday.

10:15 I tell you the truth, whoever does not receive the kingdom of God like a child will never enter it.'

Only those who receive the kingdom of God in a childlike manner will be able to enter in. This requires a humbling of ourselves; realising that like little children we are dependent on God for all that we have. Most importantly, God has provided the only way whereby we might be saved and enter heaven through his Son, the Lord Jesus Christ.

10:16 After he took the children in his arms, he placed his hands on them and blessed them.

The Lord opened his arms to embrace and bless the children. They received from him what their parents had brought them for in spite of the obstacles put in the way by the disciples.

Seeking, Finding, Losing

10:17 Now as Jesus was starting out on his way, someone ran up to him, fell on his knees, and said, 'Good teacher, what must I do to inherit eternal life?'

This verse (along with the verses in Matthew 19:16–21 and Luke 18:18–26) tells us a lot about the person who came to Jesus. The fact that he was running reveals his eagerness to find what he was seeking for; and his earnest desire to obtain it. His kneeling before the Lord indicates humility and his addressing Jesus as "good teacher" shows his willingness to learn and that he came to Jesus with an open heart, ready mind to receive whatever teaching the Lord would give to him.

Yet there is something strange about his question. He asks how he might "inherit" eternal life. Other gospels reveal that this man was young, rich and a ruler. His use of the word "inherit" may indicate that he thought he could obtain eternal life in the same way that he had obtained his riches, by inheritance from his parents; or possibly he thought that he might obtain it by good works. There are many today who believe they can obtain favour from God because they have done good works, as this young man had. But an entrance into heaven cannot be obtained in that way (Eph. 2:8–9).

10:18 Jesus said to him, 'Why do you call me good? No one is good except God alone.

Jesus answered the young man with a question of his own in order to direct his thoughts to the only one who is good, that is God. For if the young man were fully aware of what he is saying by addressing Jesus as "good" then he would know that he was addressing him as God.

10:19–20 You know the commandments: 'Do not murder, do not commit adultery, do not steal, do not give false testimony, do not defraud, honor your father and mother.' The man said to him, 'Teacher, I have wholeheartedly obeyed all these laws since my youth.'

The Lord knew that this young man understood all the demands of the law and that he had endeavoured to keep them. Nevertheless, he had not found the assurance of eternal life which he needed (Rom. 3:20; Rom. 8:3–4). If he had, he would not have come to Jesus seeking for it.

10:21 As Jesus looked at him, he felt love for him and said, 'You lack one thing. Go, sell whatever you have and give the money to the poor, and you will have treasure in heaven. Then come, follow me.'

As Jesus looked on this man he saw something that caused his heart to reach out in love towards him. Was it his eagerness, earnestness, or his openness toward the things of God? Whatever it was, Jesus also saw that there was something lacking in his life. Jesus knew that wealth was the most important thing to him; so he challenges him: if he really wanted what he was seeking for then he would need to give away all that he had to the poor. In return he would have an eternal treasure in heaven (Matt. 6:19–21). A similar attitude is necessary toward anything which we put before God in our hearts. Having disposed of his riches, the young man would be free to walk the path that Jesus would take him as his disciple.

10:22 But at this statement, the man looked sad and went away sorrowful, for he was very rich.

This young man came seeking, found the answer he was looking for and yet he chose to keep his worldly goods (which would perish), instead of grasping the opportunity to receive eternal life. This is the only man whom the Bible records as going away from Jesus sad. The Amplified N.T. says "his countenance fell and was gloomy, and he went away grieved and sorrowing, for he was holding great possessions." He was not willing to let go. Even after we have received eternal life, the Lord will continue to show us things in our lives that we put before him. He does this so that we might be willing to let them go and receive better, spiritual and eternal things in their place.

God of the Impossible

10:23 Then Jesus looked around and said to his disciples, 'How hard it is for the rich to enter the kingdom of God!'

Although Jesus knew what the final outcome of this meeting with the young man would be, he still felt sorrow because of what the young man would lose. Turning to his disciples, he expressed this sorrow by telling them how hard it is for someone who has riches to enter the kingdom of God.

10:24 The disciples were astonished at these words. But again Jesus said to them, 'Children, how hard it is to enter the kingdom of God!

The disciples were astounded at this remark, because in those days a person who was rich was considered to be blessed and in favour with God.

Some translations prefer, "how hard it is for those who trust in riches to enter the kingdom of God", suggesting that it is not the fact of being rich but the attitude of loving riches which makes it hard for some to enter the kingdom.

10:25 It is easier for a camel to go through the eye of a needle than for a rich person to enter the kingdom of God.'

It is so hard for a rich person to enter the kingdom of heaven that Jesus says it would be easier for a camel to go through the eye of a needle. Whether he meant an actual needle's eye or the little gate set within the larger gate at the entrance to the city is not really important. The point he was making concerned the impossibility of it.

10:26 They were even more astonished and said to one another, 'Then who can be saved?'

This astounded the disciples even more, for if this was so, then who could be saved?

10:27 Jesus looked at them and replied, 'This is impossible for mere humans, but not for God; all things are possible for God.'

Jesus had the answer. It was an impossible task for men but with God all things are possible. There is nothing that he cannot do. He has the power, strength and the ability—"to save to the uttermost" (Heb. 7:25); to make grace abound (2 Cor. 9:8); to fulfil promises (Rom. 4:21); to subdue all things (Phil 3:21); to guard the soul's treasure (2 Tim. 1:12); to keep from falling (Jude 1:24) and "to do exceeding abundantly above all that we ask or think" (Eph. 3:20).

Gain through Loss

10:28 Peter began to speak to him, 'Look, we have left everything to follow you!'

Peter, as spokesman for the disciples, wanted to know, since they had left it all to follow the Lord Jesus Christ (Luke 5:11), what were they going to get out of it?

10:29–30 Jesus said, 'I tell you the truth, there is no one who has left home or brothers or sisters or mother or father or children or fields for my sake and for the sake of the gospel who will not receive in this age a hundred times as much — homes, brothers, sisters, mothers, children, fields, all with persecutions — and in the age to come, eternal life.

God is a debtor to no man. No one gives up anyone, anything, or makes any sacrifice for the Lord's sake or the Gospel's without receiving in return, not just the same measure but with 10,000% interest ("a hundred times as much" actually indicates a return which cannot be measured).

When we become his follower we become part of the household—the family of God—therefore we have countless brothers and sisters, mothers, children [spiritual], (Eph. 2:19) and besides all this persecutions as well (Luke 21:12), in this life; and most importantly of all "in the age to come, eternal life".

10:31 But many who are first will be last, and the last first.'

The Lord's ways are not our ways, and so he reverses the order of what people see as important. With Jesus, the last is first and the first is last. The disciples had been the first ones called to follow Jesus, but there would be many other disciples called after them who would be preferred before them.

Third Prediction of His Death and Resurrection

10:32 They were on the way, going up to Jerusalem. Jesus was going ahead of them, and they were amazed, but those who followed were afraid. He took the twelve aside again and began to tell them what was going to happen to him.

The Lord commenced his final journey to Jerusalem, resolutely letting nothing deter him from reaching his goal (Luke 9:51). He was walking according to his Father's will and would soon become "the way" of salvation. Jesus, the good shepherd, led his disciples and they obediently followed. Even so, they were amazed or more correctly bewildered and afraid that he was heading to the place where they knew the religious leaders were waiting to take his life. It was like walking straight into a lion's den.

Perhaps the disciples had failed to understand the Lord's two previous predictions of his death; in any case, he reminds them of it again. It may have seemed to the disciples that he was walking into danger, but to Jesus who knew the plan of salvation he was walking ever closer to his final victory.

10:33–34 'Look, we are going up to Jerusalem, and the Son of Man will be handed over to the chief priests and experts in the law. They will condemn him to death and will turn him over to the Gentiles. They will mock him, spit on him, flog him severely, and kill him. Yet after three days, he will rise again.

"We are going up"—the words reveal a certain determination. For the Lord there was no other way to go; he had to reach Calvary no matter what the cost. On reaching the city he knew he would be delivered to the chief priests and the Sanhedrin who would find him guilty and condemn him (Matt. 26:57–66). They would spit in his face, mock him (Matt. 26:67–68) and hand him over to the Romans who would further mock him, scourge him and put him to death (Matt. 27:26–31). But in all this they could not triumph over him for on the third day he would rise from the dead a victor over all his foes (Mark 16:6).

Today, Jesus Christ leads all his disciples, in many various ways, to follow a path of suffering as he did, with the same determination that he had. We cannot do this in our on strength but we "can do all things through Christ who strengthens" us (Phil. 4:13).

To be Great is to be a Servant
10:35 Then James and John, the sons of Zebedee, came to him and said, 'Teacher, we want you to do for us whatever we ask.'

Matthew tells us (Matt. 20:20) that James and John's mother came with her sons to make this request of Jesus on their behalf. She wanted the best for her sons and they had an ambition to get on in the world. It is always good to have a desire to grow in grace and to receive more from God; the trouble was that James and John regarded reigning with Christ from a worldly viewpoint. Their request expressed an ambition rather than a spiritual desire. Nevertheless, they came in faith, for they had no doubt that Jesus was able to grant them whatever they asked of him.

10:36 He said to them, 'What do you want me to do for you?'

Jesus responded by giving them an open invitation to ask for what they wanted. Their request would reveal how deep or shallow their spirituality actually was. If the Lord gave us an invitation to ask whatever we wanted from him, what would we ask for? Such an invitation was also given to King Solomon (1 Kings 3:5–13).

10:37 They said to him, 'Permit one of us to sit at your right hand and the other at your left in your glory.'

The brothers' request revealed their motive to be selfish ambition. It might be that they believed Jesus was about to set up the kingdom of God on earth and wanted to secure positions of honour for themselves; their hearts were blind to the truth that Jesus was about to suffer, and they did not stop to consider this or to sympathise with him.

10:38 But Jesus said to them, 'You don't know what you are asking! Are you able to drink the cup I drink or be baptized with the baptism I experience?'

Jesus, however, did not rebuke them harshly. He realised that they had not yet fully understood the spiritual nature of his kingdom. When they did, they would be radically changed. So he used a challenging question to prepare them for the great shift in their understanding which his cross would inaugurate.

Firstly, he asked if they were able to drink of his cup. In the Old Testament, a cup was used as a symbol both for suffering, and for joy (Isa. 51:17; Ps. 23:5). Jesus would again refer to this cup in the Garden of Gethsemane (Luke 22:42). Secondly, he asked if they were able to undergo his baptism. This could be a reference to being overwhelmed by a flood, a picture of suffering in the Old Testament (Psalm 69:15). By these two questions, Jesus was examining whether James and John were willing to suffer for him and to offer up their lives as living sacrifices in service for him.

10:39 They said to him, 'We are able.' Then Jesus said to them, 'You will drink the cup I drink, and you will be baptized with the baptism I experience,

Whether they clearly understood what Jesus was asking we cannot be sure, but their answer was very bold: "we can". Surely, before the cross they could never have imagined what this would mean but the Lord knew what would lie ahead of them and what it would cost them to be his followers. In a coming day they would indeed drink of his cup and be baptised with the same baptism as he; James dying by the sword (Acts 12:2) and John exiled to Patmos (Rev. 1:9).

10:40 but to sit at my right or at my left is not mine to give. It is for those for whom it has been prepared.'

Nevertheless to grant their request to sit on his left or right was not Christ's to give; only the Father could ordain this. It was the Father who exalted Christ to the highest place (Phil. 2:9). A place beside him will be given to those for whom it is prepared. When Jesus was crucified, which certainly was a display of "the glory of God"; two thieves hung on either side of him. Did James and John then understand that being at the side of Jesus was important for every believer, and not just for a select few?

10:41 Now when the other ten heard this, they became angry with James and John.

The other ten disciples displayed their own spiritual shallowness by their anger at the two who had tried to gain an advantage over them.

10:42 Jesus called them and said to them, 'You know that those who are recognized as rulers of the Gentiles lord it over them, and those in high positions use their authority over them.

But Jesus was not angered. Instead, he used the incident to emphasise once again the new principles that would govern his spiritual kingdom. In the world of Jesus' time those who ruled the nations did so with a rod of iron, having absolute power over the people and holding them in complete subjection.

10:43–44 But it is not this way among you. Instead whoever wants to be great among you must be your servant, and whoever wants to be first among you must be the slave of all.

This pattern was not to be followed by the followers of Christ; their attitude was to be completely the reverse. It is those who become servants to all who are the greatest in Christ's kingdom; and those who slave in the interests of others are to be considered of highest importance.

10:45 For even the Son of Man did not come to be served but to serve, and to give his life as a ransom for many.'

Even Christ did not come to enjoy the service of others but took the servant's position (Phil. 2:7); paying the ransom price to redeem people back to God (1 Pet. 1:18–19).

Blind Bartimaeus—Persistency

This chapter ends by presenting Bartimaeus as an example of persistency—never giving up no matter what obstacles need to be overcome.

10:46 They came to Jericho. As Jesus and his disciples and a large crowd were leaving Jericho, Bartimaeus the son of Timaeus, a blind beggar, was sitting by the road.

Bartimaeus, being blind, was at a disadvantage to the people who crowded around Jesus. He could not get near to him; and for a while did not even know who it was who was passing by.

10:47 When he heard that it was Jesus the Nazarene, he began to shout, 'Jesus, Son of David, have mercy on me!'

When he discovered that it was Jesus of Nazareth, he used his strong voice to catch Jesus' attention. Bartimaeus recognised Jesus as the promised Messiah, calling him "Son of David" (Jer. 33:17). His pleas for mercy demonstrate that he realised that he had no rightful claims to make, and could not demand his healing.

10:48 Many scolded him to get him to be quiet, but he shouted all the more, 'Son of David, have mercy on me!'

Moreover, Bartimaeus was not put off by the attitude of the people; ignoring their objections he cried out to Jesus all the more.

10:49 Jesus stopped and said, 'Call him.' So they called the blind man and said to him, 'Have courage! Get up! He is calling you.'

If the people of Jericho had no time for Bartimaeus, Jesus did. He stopped and called for Bartimaeus to be brought to him. When the people saw Jesus' compassion and concern then their attitude changed. Jesus' presence and example made all the difference to the behaviour of the people; it still does.

10:50 He threw off his cloak, jumped up, and came to Jesus.

The man immediately responded by throwing off all that hindered him from coming to Jesus. In a similar way, those who come to Christ today must throw off the doubt, unbelief and pride which hinder their response to him.

10:51 Then Jesus said to him, 'What do you want me to do for you?' The blind man replied, 'Rabbi, let me see again.'

Although the Lord knew what Bartimaeus needed (surely it was obvious) yet he still wanted him to make his request; and he gives the same invitation to us today to ask so that we might receive (Luke 11:9).

10:52 Jesus said to him, 'Go, your faith has healed you.' Immediately he regained his sight and followed him on the road.

Because he asked in faith, believing that Jesus could completely heal him, Bartimaeus received his sight and became a follower of Jesus.

Discussion Question for Chapter 10

1. vv. 1–12. According to Jesus, how did marriage originate, and how long is it meant to last?

2. vv. 1–12. What were Jesus' view of divorce and re-marriage?

3. vv. 13–16. Are children able to enter the kingdom of God? If so, how?

4. vv. 17–27. Why do you think the young man was sad when Jesus told him that to have eternal life he must give all his money to the poor?

5. vv. 28–31. What does Jesus promise to all those who leave everything behind to follow him?

You will find suggested answers to the study questions on pages 183–193.

Mark Chapter 11

Triumphant Entry into Jerusalem

11:1–2 Now as they approached Jerusalem, near Bethphage and Bethany, at the Mount of Olives, Jesus sent two of his disciples and said to them, 'Go to the village ahead of you. As soon as you enter it, you will find a colt tied there that has never been ridden. Untie it and bring it here.

Jesus made preparation for his entry into Jerusalem by sending two of his disciples to bring the colt of an ass (Matt. 21:2) which they would find tied up at the place he specified. The unusual thing about this was that the colt had never been ridden before. Normally, such an animal might prove very difficult to ride; but Christ was able to tame the animal with a touch. In these verses we observe the omniscience (all-knowing) of Christ, which is an attribute of God. Only God could know where the colt would be, and the details of its history.

11:3 If anyone says to you, 'Why are you doing this?' 'say, 'The Lord needs it and will send it back here soon.'

Jesus also knew that the disciples would be challenged concerning their right to take the colt. Their answer, "the Lord needs it", would be sufficient for the colt to be freely given without further argument. Jesus had the absolute right to use the colt if he wished, for, "The LORD owns the earth and all it contains" (Ps. 24:1).

Some commentators take what was done to the colt as an illustration for Christian life; inasmuch as the Lord has set us free (John 8:36; Rom. 6:18) and has first claim on our lives (Rom. 14:8).

11:4–6 So they went and found a colt tied at a door, outside in the street, and untied it. Some people standing there said to them, 'What are you doing, untying that colt?' They replied as Jesus had told them, and the bystanders let them go.

Everything happened exactly as Jesus said it would; some locals challenged the disciples about their removing of the colt, but did not obstruct them when they knew that it was wanted by Jesus.

We too can be sure that if we receive any word from Christ then it will be fulfilled (Luke 21:33).

11:7 Then they brought the colt to Jesus, threw their cloaks on it, and he sat on it.

The disciples were willing to give up their coats to provide an improvised saddle and that this untamed colt was willing to submit itself under the hand of Jesus without any fuss. Are we as ready to give to Jesus and to submit our lives for his use?

11:8 Many spread their cloaks on the road and others spread branches they had cut in the fields.

If the disciples were willing to lend their coats to Jesus the people went even further, throwing their garments on the ground. Those who had no coats took what they found to hand—the branches of the trees—to lay down in honour of him; their crude equivalent of the red carpet which is laid out for royalty to walk on.

11:9–10 Both those who went ahead and those who followed kept shouting, 'Hosanna! Blessed is the one who comes in the name of the Lord! Blessed is the coming kingdom of our father David! Hosanna in the highest!'

So Jesus made his entry into Jerusalem riding on a donkey in fulfilment of the scripture (Zech. 9:9). The people welcome him as the promised deliverer or saviour ("Hosanna" means "save, we pray") and as their king (Isaiah 9:7). These could not have been the same people who would later cry out for him to be crucified, for they acknowledged that he came in the name of the Lord. Yet it may have been the case that they believed that he had come to set up his kingdom on earth; whereas in fact he had come to impart the life of his kingdom into people's hearts (Luke 17:21).

11:11 Then Jesus entered Jerusalem and went to the temple. And after looking around at everything, he went out to Bethany with the twelve since it was already late.

On entering the city Jesus went immediately to the temple to survey all that was going on there. In Matthew 21:15–16 the chief priests and scribes objected to him about the children's' praising him in the temple, but in reply Jesus quoted Psalm 8:2, "from the mouths of children and nursing babies you have ordained praise"; and in Luke 19:40 Christ insisted that if his own disciples did not praise him then the very stones would do so.

As it was already late, Jesus left the city which would have been crowded for the festival and full of his enemies to stay in the safety of a home in Bethany; probably that of Mary, Martha and Lazarus.

Barrenness

11:12 Now the next day, as they went out from Bethany, he was hungry.

Just like any other man, Jesus knew hunger and this clearly demonstrates that he was not only the divine Son of God, but also fully human—the Son of Man.

11:13 After noticing in the distance a fig tree with leaves, he went to see if he could find any fruit on it. When he came to it he found nothing but leaves, for it was not the season for figs.

Nearby was a flourishing fig tree, and so Jesus approaches it, expecting to find fruit, even though it was not the season for figs. Often before the main crop of figs the fig tree produces smaller figs, and it may have been these which Jesus hoped to find. But the tree was barren; there was no fruit on it.

If these verses are taken to be an enacted parable, then the fig tree represents Israel. God had chosen Israel to be his own people and had given them his word so that they might bear the fruit of righteousness. Yet when God sent his only Son to them, he found no such fruit, but only rejection.

11:14 He said to it, 'May no one ever eat fruit from you again.' And his disciples heard it.

It was because of its barrenness that the Lord cursed the fig tree and it died. Similar judgment would await all those who rejected Christ and failed to produce the fruits of repentance and good works motivated by faith in him.

God's desire for those he has chosen, whom he indwells by his Spirit and to whom he has given his word, is that we might bear fruit for his honour and glory (John 15:5; Rom. 7:4). In fact, as part of this on-going process, Jesus said that God will "prune" the branches of his vine (often through tribulation) so that they may bring forth even more fruit (John 15:2).

Cleansing the Temple

11:15–16 Then they came to Jerusalem. Jesus entered the temple area and began to drive out those who were selling and buying in the temple courts. He turned over the tables of the money changers and the chairs of those selling doves, and he would not permit anyone to carry merchandise through the temple courts.

When he had visited the temple on the previous day, Jesus had witnessed all that was going on there. His purpose in returning was to cleanse and purify it as a place of worship. The money changers and animal sellers occupied the court of the Gentiles, which was the part of the temple which had been set aside for those of all nations to pray to God. For Jesus the spiritual act of worship was of greater importance than the outward observance of religion, which these money makers had been taking advantage of. So he drives them out of the temple, and would not permit any merchandise in the temple area at all; bringing the area back into use for its intended purpose.

11:17 Then he began to teach them and said, 'Is it not written: 'My house will be called a house of prayer for all nations'? But you have turned it into a den of robbers!'

The fact that Jesus needed to teach the Jews this suggests that they had become so used to misusing the temple that they had forgotten its true purpose. So Jesus instructs them that the proper use of temple was as a "house of prayer" (Isa. 56:7) and that it was sacrilege to do any other business there.

11:18–19 The chief priests and the experts in the law heard it and they considered how they could assassinate him, for they feared him, because the whole crowd was amazed by his teaching. When evening came, Jesus and his disciples went out of the city.

You would have thought that the chief priest and scribes, the upholders of the Jewish religion, would have supported Jesus in this reform. Instead they tried to find a way to kill him, for they feared that the people would forsake their teachings and follow Jesus instead; in whom they saw a sincerity and truth which their leaders did not have.

Success or Failure in Prayer

11:20–21 In the morning as they passed by, they saw the fig tree withered from the roots. Peter remembered and said to him, 'Rabbi, look! The fig tree you cursed has withered.'

The following morning, as they were returning to Jerusalem from Bethany, the disciples noticed that the fig tree which Jesus had cursed was completely dead, from the roots up. Peter drew attention to this fact.

11:22 Jesus said to them, 'Have faith in God.

Jesus used the fig tree to encourage their faith and teach them how to be successful in prayer; for with God nothing is impossible. Jesus had spoken the word and it was done; even though in this instance it did not happen straight away. There is nothing that he cannot do (Mark 10:27).

Faith is the constant attitude of taking God at his word, believing without a shadow of doubt that he will do what he says (Heb. 1:1).

11:23 I tell you the truth, if someone says to this mountain, 'Be lifted up and thrown into the sea,' and does not doubt in his heart but believes that what he says will happen, it will be done for him.

Jesus stated that there is nothing impossible for those who have this kind of faith. The mountain is an immovable object, representing every problem, need, or situation that we can face. These will be completely uprooted and removed through faith alone. There must be no uncertainty in the heart: believe that what you have declared in the Lord's name will take place (Mark 9:23).

11:24 For this reason I tell you, whatever you pray and ask for, believe that you have received it, and it will be yours.

This promise still stands for all believers. Whatever we desire, so long as those desires are good, if we believe that we have received the answer to our prayer then the answer will be ours (John 15:7).

11:25–26 Whenever you stand praying, if you have anything against anyone, forgive him, so that your Father in heaven will also forgive you your sins.'

However, Jesus also wanted his disciples to avoid the pitfalls that would make their prayers unsuccessful. Although we have access to God the Father through the Lord Jesus Christ at all times (Eph. 2:18) several things can hinder our prayer life. Among them are unbelief, unconfessed sin and the one that Jesus highlighted in this passage, an unforgiving spirit. Forgiveness is the complete cancelation of sin or debt. When we remember that God has forgiven us so much, we ought not to withhold our forgiveness from others (Eph. 4:32; Col. 3:13).

Jesus said that we hold anything against anyone, when we stand praying, we must forgive, whether they are brothers and sisters in Christ or unbelievers. As we forgive so we too may receive forgiveness. This does not mean that God is ever unwilling to forgive us, for our God is ever ready to pardon (Neh. 9:17), but that our unforgiving spirit creates a barrier which prevents us receiving God's forgiveness.

If we do not forgive, and harbour bitterness in our hearts then we are not in a right place to receive from God. Our prayers will continue to go unanswered until we put things right.

Whose Authority?

11:27 They came again to Jerusalem. While Jesus was walking in the temple courts, the chief priests, the experts in the law, and the elders came up to him

Having arrived once again at Jerusalem, Jesus returned to the temple where he was immediately confronted by the chief priests and experts in the law who were on this occasion joined by the elders, the heads of the tribes and clans of the Jewish nation.

11:28 and said, 'By what authority are you doing these things? Or who gave you this authority to do these things?'

They had certainly not forgiven Jesus for what he had done in the temple the day before and challenged his authority to do such things. What kind of authority did Jesus have; was it political, religious, or military? Who gave him that authority?

11:29 Jesus said to them, 'I will ask you one question. Answer me and I will tell you by what authority I do these things:

Jesus refused to answer their question, unless they answered his question first. His question strikes at the heart of their deceit and hypocrisy. We recall that when Job questioned God, God in return questioned Job and Job had no answers to give; God silenced him.

11:30–32 John's baptism — was it from heaven or from people? Answer me.' They discussed with one another, saying, 'If we say, 'From heaven,' he will say, 'Then why did you not believe him?' But if we say, 'From people — ' (they feared the crowd, for they all considered John to be truly a prophet).

The fact that they could not answer Jesus concerning the source of John the Baptist's authority reveals what kind of men these religious leaders were. They were in a quandary—for if they admitted that John's authority came from God then Jesus would ask why they had not heeded John's message. On the other hand, if they said that John spoke of his own accord then the people would turn on them because they considered John to be a prophet.

11:33 So they answered Jesus, 'We don't know.' Then Jesus said to them, 'Neither will I tell you by what authority I am doing these things.'

So the religious leaders tried to avoid the issue by stating that they did not know, thus condemning themselves. For why were they plotting to kill Jesus, whom John had pointed them too, if they remained genuinely unsure about the origin of John's Christ-heralding ministry? In their hearts they knew full well where both Jesus' and John the Baptist's authority came from; but they did not want to admit it because that would leave them with no excuse for their rejection of Christ. Failing to answer Jesus' question, they received no direct answer from him (although, Jesus actually does answer them through a parable, that of the workers in the vineyard).

Discussion Questions for Chapter 11

1. vv. 1–11. In your own words, describe what happened as Jesus entered Jerusalem.

2. vv. 11–14 and vv. 20–26. This object lesson in faith can also be taken as a parable about those living in Jerusalem in Jesus' time. What did God expect to find in their lives, and what did Jesus find instead?

3. vv. 15–18. What angered Jesus about the market place in the temple?

4. List those things which would make the disciples prayers successful and what things would hinder their prayers.

5. vv. 27–33. Why do you think that the Pharisees questioned Jesus' authority?

You will find suggested answers to the study questions on pages 183–193.

Mark Chapter 12

Israel's Rejection of the Messiah

12:1 Then he began to speak to them in parables: 'A man planted a vineyard. He put a fence around it, dug a pit for its winepress, and built a watchtower. Then he leased it to tenant farmers and went on a journey.

The parable of the workers in the vineyard is loosely based upon Isaiah 5:1–7 and so the people, particularly the religious leaders, would almost immediately have recognized that Jesus was talking about them.

The man who planted the vineyard is a reference to God who planted Israel in the land of Canaan. He had promised this land to Abraham and his descendants (Gen. 12:6–7) and although it was many years later that the promise was fulfilled, God kept his word (2 Peter 3:8–9). After God had brought them out of Egypt he gave them the land which he had prepared (or planted) for them.

The fence around the vineyard speaks of the divine protection which was given to his people, as the angel of the Lord encamped around them (Psalm 34:7) and God was as a wall of fire around them (Zech. 2:5). The fence can also speak of separation, for God separated Israel to himself to be his holy people (Lev. 20:26) to keep his laws and walk in his ways.

The winepress might represent the temple where the people were meant to bring the fruit of the vine as part of their tithes and offerings which were made into wine. Spiritually, this may be a reference to the worship, devotion, thanksgiving, and offerings of Israel. The tower (a place of defence) was the city of Jerusalem itself.

The owner of the vineyard leased it to tenants, and God gave his land, his laws, his protection and his promises to Israel that they might be his stewards. The vineyard owner left the tenants to care for the vineyard and produce its fruit until he returned. Believers are to be good stewards of all that God has entrusted to us until he returns in the person of Christ (Luke 19:13; 1 Cor. 6:20; 1 Pet. 4:10). However Israel had failed their trust. They had not kept the covenant which God had made with them; they broke his laws, mixing with the heathen in the land and serving their idols.

12:2–5 At harvest time he sent a slave to the tenants to collect from them his portion of the crop. But those tenants seized his slave, beat him, and sent him away empty-handed. So he sent another slave to them again. This one they struck on the head and treated outrageously. He sent another and that one they killed. This happened to many others, some of whom were beaten, others killed.

When it was harvest time, the vineyard owner sent his servants to receive his rightful share of the fruit of his vineyard. But the tenants refused to hand it over and beat the servants, sending some away empty handed, and killing others.

In a similar way, God had sent his prophets to call Israel to bring him his rightful dues of love, obedience and worship. Again and again they rejected, beat and killed his prophets; yet God in his mercy and longsuffering did not reject or give up on these wicked people. He sent more prophets, inviting the people to repent and receive forgiveness; but they would not listen and killed these also (Heb. 11:36–37).

12:6 He had one left, his one dear son. Finally he sent him to them, saying, 'They will respect my son.'

Finally, the owner sent his only son to the tenants, thinking that they would respect him. In the same way God sent his only begotten Son, whom he loved, the Lord Jesus Christ (Heb. 1:1–2). Here he was, addressing the scribes and Pharisees, and surely if these religious leaders were sincere in their worship of God as they professed to be, then surely they would respect and honour his Son.

12:7–8 But those tenants said to one another, 'This is the heir. Come, let's kill him and the inheritance will be ours!' So they seized him, killed him, and threw his body out of the vineyard.

The tenants of the vineyard recognised the son of the owner. Jesus may be implying that although they refused to acknowledge it, in their hearts the Pharisees knew him to be speaking the truth that he was God's Son. Nevertheless, they rejected him (John 1:11). They took him to be crucified outside the city walls so that they may keep the inheritance (the nation of Israel) for themselves.

12:9 What then will the owner of the vineyard do? He will come and destroy those tenants and give the vineyard to others.

Because of Israel's rejection of Christ they became blinded and were cut off from receiving the salvation which he came to give (Rom. 11:7). Within a generation of Jesus uttering these words, Jerusalem and its temple were destroyed by Roman armies. Yet through their rejection a way was made for the Gentiles to receive salvation (Rom. 11:15). Moreover, this blindness of the Jews is only temporary; it will remain only until the full number of the Gentiles is gathered in (Rom. 11:25).

12:10 Have you not read this scripture: 'The stone the builders rejected has become the cornerstone.

This verse is a quote from Psalm 118:22. The "builders" are the leaders of Israel and the "stone" is Jesus Christ whom they rejected but whom God exalted (Phil. 2:9; Rev. 5:12).

Rightful Ownership

12:11–13 This is from the Lord, and it is marvellous in our eyes'?' Now they wanted to arrest him (but they feared the crowd), because they realized that he told this parable against them. So they left him and went away. Then they sent some of the Pharisees and Herodians to trap him with his own words.

The Pharisees and Herodians were bitter enemies but they joined together for the purpose of entrapping and destroying Jesus.

12:14 When they came they said to him, 'Teacher, we know that you are truthful and do not court anyone's favour, because you show no partiality but teach the way of God in accordance with the truth. Is it right to pay taxes to Caesar or not? Should we pay or shouldn't we?'

They decided to approach Jesus with flattering words. Although they described him as "truthful" they did not acknowledge him to be the truth (John 14:6). They flattered him for being without personal prejudice and for speaking the truth about God (even though they did not believe or obey this truth).

Their question concerned the matter of paying tribute to Rome: "Is it right to give taxes to Caesar?" they asked.

12:15 But he saw through their hypocrisy and said to them, 'Why are you testing me? Bring me a denarius and let me look at it.'

Jesus knew what they were doing and saw through their hypocrisy. The fact that he asked *them* to produce a denarius is not insignificant, for it shows that although they were Jews, deriding the Roman money as idolatrous, yet they were using the coin of the Roman Empire for their business transactions.

12:16–17 So they brought one, and he said to them, 'Whose image is this, and whose inscription?' They replied, 'Caesar's.' Then Jesus said to them, 'Give to Caesar the things that are Caesar's, and to God the things that are God's.' And they were utterly amazed at him.

Jesus' answer made reference to the markings on the coin. Since Caesar's head and name were engraved on the coin, it clearly belonged to him. People, on the other hand, bear the image of God, being made in his likeness (Gen. 1:26) and so Jesus concluded that we must give to Caesar what is Caesar's (his money) and to God what is God's—ourselves (Rom. 12:1).

The Resurrection

12:18 Sadducees (who say there is no resurrection) also came to him and asked him,

After the Pharisees and Herodians had failed to trap Jesus, the Sadducees decided to try. These were a religious party who rejected any belief in life after death, resurrection, angels or spirits (Acts 23:8).

12:19–23 'Teacher, Moses wrote for us: 'If a man's brother dies and leaves a wife but no children, that man must marry the widow and father children for his brother.' There were seven brothers. The first one married, and when he died he had no children. The second married her and died without any children, and likewise the third. None of the seven had children. Finally, the woman died too. In the resurrection, when they rise again, whose wife will she be? For all seven had married her.'

So they came to Jesus, not with an enquiring mind, but with a ridiculous hypothetical situation in order to discredit him. If a woman had married seven times in the way they described (Deut. 25:5–6), whose wife would she be after the resurrection?

12:24 Jesus said to them, 'Aren't you deceived for this reason, because you don't know the scriptures or the power of God?

Jesus replied that these so called experts in the law had no understanding of the word of God (1 Tim. 1:7) and were completely ignorant of his power.

12:25 For when they rise from the dead, they neither marry nor are given in marriage, but are like angels in heaven.

The resurrection body will be different in quality to the earthly body. It will be heavenly, incorruptible and immortal (1 Cor. 15:42–44, 49) like Christ's resurrection body (Phil. 3:21). There will be no gender distinction in heaven and so there will be no marriage or sexual intercourse. These Sadducees did not appreciate God's power was able to raise up and change the body in this way (1 Cor. 6:14).

12:26–27 Now as for the dead being raised, have you not read in the book of Moses, in the passage about the bush, how God said to him, 'I am the God of Abraham, the God of Isaac, and the God of Jacob'? He is not the God of the dead but of the living. You are badly mistaken!'

Jesus further pointed out to the Sadducees that their position contradicted the writings of Moses. He referred them to Exodus 3:6 where God spoke of himself as the "I am", not the "I was", "the God of Abraham, Isaac and Jacob". These men had already been dead for some time before God spoke these words to Moses. Hence God declares himself to be not the God of the dead but of the living!

The Greatest Commandment

12:28 Now one of the experts in the law came and heard them debating. When he saw that Jesus answered them well, he asked him, 'Which commandment is the most important of all?'

The experts in the law were not a separate religious party but were interpreters of law. One such expert was impressed by the way that Jesus had answered his opponents, and so asked a question which may have been intended to probe whether Jesus upheld the true religion. Which is the greatest commandment?

12:29–30 Jesus answered, 'The most important is: 'Listen, Israel, the Lord our God, the Lord is one. Love the Lord your God with all your heart, with all your soul, with all your mind, and with all your strength.'

In reply Jesus quoted Deuteronomy 6:4–5. God is one God and there is no other God besides him. He is to be loved with the whole heart, soul mind and strength. The heart is the seat of the affections; our emotions and will. The soul is the very life of a person. The mind is the centre of understanding; and "strength" is a reference to all a person's physical abilities. This is the first and greatest commandment; and yet Jesus links it closely to the second.

12:31 The second is: 'Love your neighbour as yourself.' There is no other commandment greater than these.'

Those who fulfil the first commandment will also fulfil the second one—to love our neighbour as ourselves (Lev. 19:18). We cannot say we love God and hate a person who is made in God's image. So Jesus unites the two commandments as one for he says "there is no other *commandment* [singular] greater than these".

12:32–33 The expert in the law said to him, 'That is true, Teacher; you are right to say that he is one, and there is no one else besides him. And to love him with all your heart, with all your mind, and with all your strength and to love your neighbour as yourself is more important than all burnt offerings and sacrifices.'

The scribe is overwhelmed by Jesus' answer and expresses not only his admiration but also his agreement; for he too considered keeping this command to be far more acceptable to God than all the offerings and sacrifices that have ever been made (1 Sam. 15:22).

12:34 When Jesus saw that he had answered thoughtfully, he said to him, 'You are not far from the kingdom of God.' Then no one dared any longer to question him.

When Jesus perceived that the man answered carefully and sensibly he told him that he was near to the kingdom of God. We do not know if he ever accepted Jesus as Saviour, although a number of scribes did.

After this encounter, Jesus' opponents remained silent, for they did not dare to ask him anything more.

He is Lord

12:35–37 While Jesus was teaching in the temple courts, he said, 'How is it that the experts in the law say that the Christ is David's son? David himself, by the Holy Spirit, said, 'The Lord said to my lord, 'Sit at my right hand, until I put your enemies under your feet.'' If David himself calls him 'Lord,' how can he be his son?' And the large crowd was listening to him with delight.

Jesus now asks a question of them concerning the teaching of the scribes who said that Christ was the son of David. How can this be when David himself, inspired by the Holy Spirit, declared that the Lord (Jehovah God) said to his Lord (that is, David's Lord, the Christ) sit at my right hand until I make your enemies a footstool under you (Ps.110:1)? If David calls the Christ his own Lord then how can he be David's son? He must surely be someone greater than David.

An Outward Show of Godliness

12:38–40 In his teaching Jesus also said, 'Watch out for the experts in the law. They like walking around in long robes and elaborate greetings in the marketplaces, and the best seats in the synagogues and the places of honor at banquets. They devour widows' property, and as a show make long prayers. These men will receive a more severe punishment.'

In these verses Jesus warns against those who make a big demonstration of their piety whilst in reality their godliness is mere play acting (2 Tim. 3:5). The experts in the law were like this—they loved to dress in flowing robes as a mark of their office and to get reverential greetings in the public places, in the front seats in the synagogues and the places of honour at feasts. They revelled in earthly honour. Yet for all their devout appearance they were unscrupulous, with no moral principles. They robbed the widows of their homes (perhaps they were involved in money lending) and to cover up their greed said long prayers. Because of their hypocrisy they would receive the heavier sentence of condemnation.

Giving All

12:41–44 Then he sat down opposite the offering box, and watched the crowd putting coins into it. Many rich people were throwing in large amounts. And a poor widow came and put in two small copper coins, worth less than a penny. He called his disciples and said to them, 'I tell you the truth, this poor widow has put more into the offering box than all the others. For they all gave out of their wealth. But she, out of her poverty, put in what she had to live on, everything she had.'

Perhaps it was not by chance that Mark includes this incident of the widow casting in her mites after Jesus' statement about the experts in the law oppressing widows. Jesus might have been already sat near the place where the offerings were put when he gave his earlier warning about the experts in the law.

Jesus noticed how the rich gave out of their wealth; they could give much and have plenty left over. But he took even more notice of one poor widow woman who gave an apparently insignificant amount. Jesus knew that out of her poverty she had given all that she had to God. There is nothing anyone may do for God that is beneath his notice. It is not the amount we give to God that matters, but our willingness and the act of faith in giving, trusting that he will supply all our needs in Christ Jesus (Phil. 4:19). Since God so loved the world that he gave his Son, what ought we to give in return?

Discussion Questions for Chapter 12

1. vv. 1–12. In your own words, explain what you think this parable means.

2. vv. 13–17. Why should the Christian pay taxes to the state? (See also Romans 13:1–7)

3. vv. 28–34. According to Jesus, what is the greatest commandment?

4. vv. 35–37. Whose Son is the Christ? See also Psalm 2:7, 2 Sam. 7:14 and Psalm 45:6.

5. vv. 12:41–44. Why was the widow's offering worth more to God than all the others?

You will find suggested answers to the study questions on pages 183–193.

Mark Chapter 13

Do Not Trust in Earthly Things

13:1 Now as Jesus was going out of the temple courts, one of his disciples said to him, 'Teacher, look at these tremendous stones and buildings!'

As Jesus was leaving the temple one of his disciples was very impressed by its greatness and splendour and drew his attention to it. This was the second temple which by this time had been rebuilt and enlarged by Herod the Great. In Luke 21:5 we are told that it was adorned with shapely and magnificent stones. The Jews were very proud of it and this disciple was too.

13:2 Jesus said to him, 'Do you see these great buildings? Not one stone will be left on another. All will be torn down!'

However, if he thought to make an impression on Jesus he was greatly mistaken; Jesus was not taken up with the temporary things of this world, not even the temple. He directed this disciple's thoughts away from the temporal to the eternal (2 Cor. 4:18) by warning that what seemed so magnificent would not endure. The temple would be completely destroyed, with every stone thrown down; this took place AD 70 when the Roman legions besieged and captured Jerusalem.

The temple belonged to the old covenant; but when Jesus died and rose again this was the beginning of the new covenant. The continual animal sacrifices made in the temple were no longer required, as Jesus had made his once and for all sacrifice on the cross (Heb. 10:9–12). Jesus wanted to prepare his disciples for the day when the external regulations for worshipping God would be done away with and they would instead worship him in spirit and truth (John 4:21–24). Believers today must also be careful not to be so caught up with the external observances of Christianity that they become distracted from Christ himself (Col. 3:2).

Signs of the End of the World

13:3–4 So while he was sitting on the Mount of Olives opposite the temple, Peter, James, John, and Andrew asked him privately, 'Tell us, when will these things happen? And what will be the sign that all these things are about to take place?'

As Jesus sat on the Mount of Olives opposite the temple with just four of his disciples (Andrew is an addition to the usual three), they asked him what signs would indicate the time when these things would happen.

13:5–6 Jesus began to say to them, 'Watch out that no one misleads you. Many will come in my name, saying, 'I am he,' and they will mislead many.

The signs given in these verses were to be fulfilled from the time of the first disciples right up to the time of Jesus' return. The first was the appearance of false Christs and false teachers (claiming to represent Christ). Believers must be very careful not to be deceived by anyone (2 Thess. 2:3). The best way to safeguard ourselves is to walk close to Jesus every day, reading his word and taking it into our hearts.

Down through the centuries right up to the present time there have been many false teachers and false Christs. Their numbers will continue to increase as a sign of the near return of Jesus (1 John 2:18).

13:7 When you hear of wars and rumours of wars, do not be alarmed. These things must happen, but the end is still to come.

Jesus next refers to wars and rumours of wars; the latter being a reference to civil unrest, or acts of terrorism. Christians are not to be alarmed by these events, for we are not like those who have no hope; they are signs that our Lord's coming is getting nearer! But, says Jesus, these events do not mean that the end will come at once.

13:8 For nation will rise up in arms against nation, and kingdom against kingdom. There will be earthquakes in various places, and there will be famines. These are but the beginning of birth pains.

Whole nations shall make war against each other and earthquakes will occur in all sorts of places, even where they had previously been unknown. There will be constant famines and catastrophic happenings throughout the world. All this is but the beginnings of the sufferings that are to happen (Rom. 8:22–23).

13:9 'You must watch out for yourselves. You will be handed over to councils and beaten in the synagogues. You will stand before governors and kings because of me, as a witness to them.

Another sign of the coming end of the age is the persecution of the church. Jesus warns that his followers would be turned over to the local governing authorities to be beaten, and even appear on trial before rulers, such as when Paul appeared before Caesar (Acts 25:11–12); though this would become an opportunity for the believers to testify of Christ. Such persecution has continued throughout the Christian era and will do so until Jesus comes again. As with all the signs of the end of the age, the persecution will get worse as the end approaches.

13:10 First the gospel must be preached to all nations.

God has purposed that the message of salvation must be declared to all nations before the second coming of Christ.

13:11 When they arrest you and hand you over for trial, do not worry about what to speak. But say whatever is given you at that time, for it is not you speaking, but the Holy Spirit.

Jesus gave these instructions to his disciples concerning how they should conduct themselves when they were delivered to those in authority for the gospel's sake. These instructions hold good for believers facing persecution today. We are not to be anxious about what we are to say or try to prepare our defence beforehand, for when the time comes the Holy Spirit will speak through us.

13:12 Brother will hand over brother to death, and a father his child. Children will rise against parents and have them put to death.

Jesus further warns that close family members would betray Christians, even if that meant them being put to death.

13:13 You will be hated by everyone because of my name. But the one who endures to the end will be saved.

The time would come when all Christians would be hated and detested by the whole world for Christ's sake. Once again, the picture Jesus gives implies that this hatred would increase toward the end of the age. Nevertheless, "those who patiently endures to the end shall be made a partaker of the salvation of Christ and delivered from spiritual death' (Amp. N. T.) The Christian "must hold fast to the very end: and if he be truly Christian he will hold fast, because God holds him fast" (Alan Cole). Jesus said "remain faithful even to the point of death, and I will give you the crown that is life itself" (Rev. 2:10).

A Time of Great Trouble

13:14–18 'But when you see the abomination of desolation standing where it should not be (let the reader understand), then those in Judea must flee to the mountains. The one on the roof must not come down or go inside to take anything out of his house. The one in the field must not turn back to get his cloak. Woe to those who are pregnant and to those who are nursing their babies in those days! Pray that it may not be in winter.

Remember that Jesus was replying to his disciples' question about the signs of the end of the age when he spoke of this "abomination of desolation" (Daniel 9:27). It is difficult to see how Jesus' words could be taken as a reference to the destruction of Jerusalem by Titus, for many of the events depicted in later verses did not coincide with the Roman siege. Perhaps the "abomination" is a reference to the image of "the beast", a world-ruling opponent of Christ who would appear toward the end of time and erect a statue of himself in the temple, proclaiming himself to be God (Revelation 13:12–15; 2 Thess. 2:4). Similar profanities had defamed the temple previously. During the period of Antiochus Epiphanes a statue was erected of him in the temple and pigs were sacrificed there. But Jesus was clearly speaking here of a future day that would be worse than the time of Antiochus.

Jesus' words were given as a warning to those alive at the time of this "abomination". When they saw these things happen it would be vital for them to escape from Jerusalem and the surrounding area as quickly as possible and head for the Judean Mountains. There would be no time to take any possessions, just enough time to flee for their lives.

13:19 For in those days there will be suffering unlike anything that has happened from the beginning of the creation that God created until now, or ever will happen.

Although the days of the Roman siege were dreadful they did not come up to what Jesus foretold here. He was warning about a time of affliction that would be more dreadful than anything ever seen on earth, and which would never be witnessed again. This can only be a reference to the end of the age, a time which is spoken of in more detail in the book of the Revelation.

13:20 And if the Lord had not cut short those days, no one would be saved. But because of the elect, whom he chose, he has cut them short.

The word "elect" (chosen) is often used of believers in Christ (1 Pet. 1:2). Yet the word is also used to denote the nation of Israel. In context, Jesus has been addressing a localised situation ("let those who are in

Judea") at a particular time. It is possible that he simply means only a few will be saved alive at this time; he does not elucidate as to whether they are Christians or Jews. But given their locality, they would more likely be Jews.

13:21–22 Then if anyone says to you, 'Look, here is the Christ!' or 'Look, there he is!' do not believe him. For false messiahs and false prophets will appear and perform signs and wonders to deceive, if possible, the elect.

During these days of suffering many false prophets will appear professing to be the Christ. Many will follow and support these false prophets. They will be able to show signs and work mighty miracles (Rev. 13:11–14). These signs and miracles will be such a good counterfeit that if it was at all possible even those chosen by God would be deceived by them.

13:23 Be careful! I have told you everything ahead of time.

It is because Jesus has forewarned us of this that we can be on our guard and not taken in by what is false.

Second Coming of Christ

13:24 'But in those days, after that suffering, the sun will be darkened and the moon will not give its light; the stars will be falling from heaven, and the powers in the heavens will be shaken.

Immediately after these days of suffering are completed, awesome signs from God will appear in the heavens to announce the end of the world. Even the sun, moon and stars, together with the powers of heaven (e.g. gravity) will be shaken.

It is noteworthy that the signs given in this verse seem to correspond with those in Revelation 6:12–13, which occur at the opening of the sixth seal. Just before this, in Revelation 6:10–11 many Christians who had been martyred ask Jesus how long it will be until they are avenged. The Lord answers that it will not be until more of their fellow servants have been killed as they were. This might suggest that up until the opening of the sixth seal the church is present on the earth, whilst after the sixth seal comes the day of wrath (Rev. 6:17). On the other hand, some commentators believe the church will be removed before the great trouble occurs and "the beast" is revealed. Certainly, at some time between the sixth and seventh seal being opened the tribes of Israel are sealed (Rev. 7:1–8) and the redeemed of the Lord are in heaven (Rev. 7:9–17).

13:26–27 Then everyone will see the Son of Man arriving in the clouds with great power and glory. Then he will send angels and they will gather his elect from the four winds, from the ends of the earth to the ends of heaven.

After these signs appear in the heavens, Jesus himself will be revealed, coming in the clouds of the sky with great power and glory. Then shall be gathered in from all over the earth to the utmost limits of heaven all those who belong to him (1 Thess. 4:16–17).

Parable of the Fig Tree

13:28 'Learn this parable from the fig tree: Whenever its branch becomes tender and puts out its leaves, you know that summer is near.

This is a simple parable taking an object of nature that responds to the seasons as a matter of course. As summer approaches the young shoots appear and its leaves begin to bud. This is invariably taken as a sign that summer has arrived.

13:29 So also you, when you see these things happening, know that he is near, right at the door.

So it is with the signs the Lord gave to his disciples: they herald that his coming is near, even on the threshold

13:30 I tell you the truth, this generation will not pass away until all these things take place.

The generation here certainly does not mean that of the twelve disciples. It may refer to the generation that is alive at the time when all these signs have been accomplished. Jesus is emphasising by this and the following verse that an end will come to the world.

13:31 Heaven and earth will pass away, but my words will never pass away.

Yet although heaven and earth will perish and pass away (2 Pet. 3:10), there are some things, which, according to the eternal word of God will endure forever.

The Time of His Coming

13:32 'But as for that day or hour no one knows it — neither the angels in heaven, nor the Son — except the Father.

This verse has always presented a real difficulty in as much as if Christ is the divine son of God, how can he speak of not knowing the day of his return? Yet this difficulty might be explained if we remember that Jesus was also a man, and as a child he grew in wisdom, and in his humbles state as a man he might claim to not know something.

The point of what Jesus is saying, however, is that if he and the angels do not know the time or date of his coming, no man should presume to know it.

13:33 Watch out! Stay alert! For you do not know when the time will come.

Instead of guessing the time for the Lord's coming, Christians should be constantly on the alert, on our guard spiritually by watching that our lives stay pleasing to God and by praying, so that we might be ready when he comes.

13:34 It is like a man going on a journey. he left his house and put his slaves in charge, assigning to each his work, and commanded the doorkeeper to stay alert.

Jesus likens himself to a master who goes on a journey and puts his servants in charge of particular tasks. We are all his servants, and we are also all like the doorkeeper who was commanded to remain alert, watching for his master's return (see also Luke 19:13; 1 Cor. 15:58).

13:35–37 Stay alert, then, because you do not know when the owner of the house will return — whether during evening, at midnight, when the rooster crows, or at dawn — or else he might find you asleep when he returns suddenly. What I say to you I say to everyone: Stay alert!'

Jesus repeats his warning that since we do not know when he will return we must be watchful at all times; keeping our minds on him and doing the work he has entrusted to us. Otherwise when he comes he may find us asleep like the unbelievers; that is, in a state of spiritual apathy and dull to the things of God (Rom. 13:11; 1 Thess. 5:6). That is why he addresses his warning to all; it is not only his existing followers which must learn to be awake and watching. The teaching of Christ's second coming has led many to personal faith in him.

Discussion Questions for Chapter 13

1. vv. 5–6. Why can the reader be assured that anyone on earth claiming to be Christ is false? In answering this question, consider also how Jesus describes His own return in 13:26.

2. vv. 3–25. List some of the signs of Jesus' coming given in this chapter.

3. vv. 14–22. Describe the time of great trouble which Jesus refers to in these verses.

4. vv. 28–31. What is Jesus teaching through the parable of the fig tree?

5. vv. 32–37. Why can no one correctly predict the time of Jesus' coming?

You will find suggested answers to the study questions on pages 183–193.

Mark Chapter 14

The Plot Against Jesus

14:1 Two days before the Passover and the Feast of Unleavened Bread, the chief priests and the experts in the law were trying to find a way to arrest Jesus by stealth and kill him.

Although the religious leaders in Jerusalem had been talking for some time about ridding themselves of Jesus it was not until two days before the Passover that they met together to plan on how they could bring about his death by deceptive means. That they sought to do this by stealth reveals that they knew they had no justification for their actions.

14:2 For they said, 'Not during the feast, so there won't be a riot among the people.'

They originally hoped, however, to put the plan on hold until after the Passover, in case it caused uproar among the people, with whom Jesus was very popular. So they planned to take Jesus after the feast, until circumstances caused them to change their plans. In fact, it was God's own plan that was about to be fulfilled in Jerusalem (Prov. 19:21; Psalm 33:11).

Jesus Anointed

14:3 Now while Jesus was in Bethany at the house of Simon the leper, reclining at the table, a woman came with an alabaster jar of costly aromatic oil from pure nard. After breaking open the jar, she poured it on his head.

This event took place in Bethany where Jesus often resorted when going to Jerusalem. This time the supper was held in Simon the leper's house; since Simon was present he had obviously been healed by the Lord. The differences between Matthew (Matt. 26:6–13) and Mark's account of this anointing and that of John (John 12:1–8) might readily be explained if we assume that Martha and Mary had prepared supper in Simon's house. Matthew and Mark place this event two days before the Passover; whereas John mentions Jesus arriving in Bethany six days before the Passover. But we have already seen in Mark that Jesus spent several days in Bethany before his execution, and so although he arrived six days before, the anointing may well have taken place (as Mark relates) two days before the Passover.

Although Mark does not name her, John affirms that is was Mary the sister of Lazarus who poured a liquid perfume made out of pure nard on Jesus' feet (nard was extracted from the spikenard plant). It was very costly and highly prized, being imported from Arabia, India and the Far East. Since Mary was someone who listened attentively to Jesus' words (Luke 10:39), had she saved the perfume purposely, realising that she was anointing Christ for his burial; or did she act in ignorant devotion? She did not keep anything for herself but gave it all to Jesus. Mark says that Mary anointed Jesus' head whilst John mentions his feet. It is quite likely that Mary (who had come to anoint his body for burial) would have anointed both.

14:4–5 But some who were present indignantly said to one another, 'Why this waste of expensive ointment? It could have been sold for more than three hundred silver coins and the money given to the poor!' So they spoke angrily to her.

The act of worship which expressed Mary's love for the Lord brought an angry response from the onlookers, including the twelve disciples. They all sharply criticised Mary. To them it was a complete waste of an expensive item which could have been used for better things. Their minds were still fixed on material benefits and so they were blinded to the spiritual significance of what Mary had done. In any case after all that Jesus had done for them should they begrudge him this honour? In John's gospel we are told that it was Judas Iscariot that made the most objections, since he been stealing from the purse he had been entrusted with (John 12:6).

14:6 But Jesus said, 'Leave her alone. Why are you bothering her? She has done a good service for me.

Jesus knew what was in Mary's heart and comes to her defence, rebuking the disciples for accusing her. He commends Mary for her act of faith, declaring it to be good and beautiful as an expression of love.

14:7 For you will always have the poor with you, and you can do good for them whenever you want. But you will not always have me!

Mary seemed to understand something that the disciples had not, although Jesus had repeatedly told them about it: he was leaving them. In fact his hour had almost come; now was the time to do something for him. There would always be poor people in the world for whom they could give help at any time.

14:8 She did what she could. She anointed my body beforehand for burial.

Jesus informs them quite clearly that she had anointed him for his burial.

14:9 I tell you the truth, wherever the gospel is proclaimed in the whole world, what she has done will also be told in memory of her.'

Jesus said that Mary's act of devotion would be remembered as a testimony to her wherever the gospel was preached. In other words, her actions are worthy of being commended as an example for all believers to follow—symbolising the surrender of their all to the Lord.

Judas Agrees to Betray Jesus

14:10–11 Then Judas Iscariot, one of the twelve, went to the chief priests to betray Jesus into their hands. When they heard this, they were delighted and promised to give him money. So Judas began looking for an opportunity to betray him.

After this incident Judas Iscariot wasted no time. He had made up his mind to betray Jesus into the hands of his enemies and so conspired with the chief priests how he might betray him into their hands without the people knowing. They rejoiced to hear this, since this is what they had been waiting for. Who better to help them than one who was his disciple and professed friend (Psalm 41:9; Psalm 55:12–14)? The price that they would pay Judas for the life of the Lord was thirty pieces of silver, the price of a slave.

The Preparation for the Passover

14:12 Now on the first day of the feast of Unleavened Bread, when the Passover lamb is sacrificed, Jesus' disciples said to him, 'Where do you want us to prepare for you to eat the Passover?'

When the disciples asked Jesus where he wanted them to prepare for the Passover, they found that God had already made preparations of his own.

14:13 He sent two of his disciples and told them, 'Go into the city, and a man carrying a jar of water will meet you. Follow him.

As they entered Jerusalem they would meet a man carrying a pitcher of water, an uncommon sight enough, as it was usually the women or children who did this. He would lead them to the place which God had ordained for this last supper. Mark seems eager to affirm that God was not leaving any of the events surrounding his Son's last days to chance.

14:14–15 Wherever he enters, tell the owner of the house, 'The Teacher says, 'Where is my guest room where I may eat the Passover with my disciples?' He will show you a large room upstairs, furnished and ready. Make preparations for us there.

God had also prepared the owner of the house to receive the disciples, and when they arrived he guided them to an upper room which was already prepared for the Passover celebration.

14:16–18 So the disciples left, went into the city, and found things just as he had told them, and they prepared the Passover. Then, when it was evening, he came to the house with the twelve. While they were at the table eating, Jesus said, 'I tell you the truth, one of you eating with me will betray me.'

The disciples obeyed Jesus without any questions and it found things to be exactly as he had told them. So they prepared the Passover ready for his arrival. When we do exactly as Jesus commands us we will find that all things will work out right.

At evening time, Jesus arrived with the rest of the twelve, and as they sat down to eat, he dropped the first bomb shell of the evening. One of the twelve, one of those closest to him, was going to betray him. We cannot imagine what a shock this must have been to the disciples; all except one.

14:19 They were distressed, and one by one said to him, 'Surely not I?'

The disciples began to show their sadness at hearing this news; yet it is significant to notice that they did not ask "who is it?" or insist that "it isn't me". Their hearts had been so pierced by Jesus' words that even the innocent among them began to examine themselves, and asked him one by one "is it I?"

14:20 He said to them, 'It is one of the twelve, one who dips his hand with me into the bowl.

In reply, Jesus did not openly name the betrayer, but gives an almost "cryptic clue" so that the person himself would know that Jesus was not ignorant of his plans. According to John 13:26, it is possible that only John saw who dipped his hand in the dish at the same time as Jesus, and so understood the betrayer to be Judas Iscariot.

14:21 For the Son of Man will go as it is written about him, but woe to that man by whom the Son of Man is betrayed! It would be better for him if he had never been born.'

The fact that every minute detail of the plan of salvation was foreordained by God did not absolve Judas Iscariot from blame for the part which he played in it. Like any other person, Judas had a free will; he did not have to betray Jesus. Jesus gave him plenty of opportunities to repent but he continually hardened his heart. Therefore he would pay the dreadful penalty for his actions and there would never be a rest for his soul. That is why Jesus said, "It would be better for him if he had never been born".

14:22–26 While they were eating, he took bread, and after giving thanks he broke it, gave it to them, and said, 'Take it. This is my body.' And after taking the cup and giving thanks, he gave it to them, and they all drank from it. He said to them, 'This is my blood, the blood of the covenant that is poured out for many. I tell you the truth; I will no longer drink of the fruit of the vine until that day when I drink it new in the kingdom of God.' After singing a hymn, they went out to the Mount of Olives.

Judas having left, Jesus proceeded to institute a new memorial—the communion—to replace that of the Passover. Just as the Passover involved the death and blood of a lamb, so the memorial Christ instituted would point to his own broken body and to his blood shed on the cross. As Passover commemorated the Jews' deliverance from slavery to Egypt, so the communion pictures the deliverance which Christ provided (through his death) from the slavery of sin. Christ gave himself for us that we might be redeemed, purchased for God by his blood. This blessing of redemption is closely related to the forgiveness of sins (Eph. 1:7).

The Passover provided a number of types and pictures of the reality which was soon to be fulfilled by Christ's death, and which thereafter would no longer be needed. Christ would never take Passover again, but he would share the blessings of the redemption which it symbolised with all the believers in his kingdom. Barnes says, "The observance of the Passover, and of the rites shadowing forth future things, here end...The design of all these types and shadows is about to be accomplished...Hereafter, when my Father's kingdom is established in heaven, we will partake together of the thing represented by these types and ceremonial observances - the blessings and triumphs of redemption."

Before facing his last and fiercest battle at the cross, Jesus paused to sing hymns of praise to God with his disciples. It is commonly accepted that the hymns sung by Jews on such an occasion were the Hallel, or Psalm 113–118. In Christ's singing there was a note of praise for the victory which he was about to accomplish. Following the hymn, they set out for the Mount of Olives, where in a garden called Gethsemane, they often met to pray.

14:26–31 Then Jesus said to them, 'You will all fall away, for it is written, 'I will strike the shepherd, and the sheep will be scattered.' But after I am raised, I will go ahead of you into Galilee.' Peter said to him, 'Even if they all fall away, I will not!' Jesus said to him, 'I tell you the truth, today—this very night—before a rooster crows twice, you will deny me three times.' But Peter insisted emphatically, 'Even if I must die with you, I will never deny you.' And all of them said the same thing.

The Old Testament had predicted the scattering of Christ's disciples at the time of his arrest and crucifixion. But Jesus introduced a new reality— he would gather them to himself again after he was raised from the dead. All the disciples, including Peter, were indignant at the suggestion that they would forsake their Lord. They overestimated their own ability and loyalty; though Jesus' ability to keep his word was never in doubt.

14:32–41 Then they went to a place called Gethsemane, and Jesus said to his disciples, 'Sit here while I pray.' He took Peter, James, and John with him, and became very troubled and distressed. He said to them, 'My soul is deeply grieved, even to the point of death. Remain here and stay alert.' Going a little farther, he threw himself to the ground and prayed that if it were possible the hour would pass from him. He said, 'Abba, Father, all things are possible for you. Take this cup away from me. Yet not what I will, but what you will.' Then he came and found them sleeping, and said to Peter, 'Simon, are you sleeping? Couldn't you stay awake for one hour? Stay awake and pray that you will not fall into temptation. The spirit is willing, but the flesh is weak.' He went away again and prayed the same thing. When he came again he found them sleeping; they could not keep their eyes open. And they did not know what to tell him. He came a third time and said to them, 'Are you still sleeping and resting? Enough of that! The hour has come. Look, the Son of Man is betrayed into the hands of sinners.

As Christ approached the garden of Gethsemane, he began to enter his agony, an agony which only he could face. The sorrow itself was sufficient to kill him (v. 34). Asking all his disciples, some further off and some nearby, to pray with him, he fell on his face to intercede with God for the last time as a man; asking that if it were possible, the hour might pass from him. It was certainly possible, for Christ would not be forced to suffer and die for the sin of the world. Yet it was the only way for lost sinners to be redeemed for God; their redemption by any other means was impossible. The salvation of sinners was the purpose for which Christ had come into the world (1 Tim. 1:15; John 3:16). Realising this, despite the agony of the moment, Christ purposed to go through with the plan—not for his own sake, but for ours. He prayed, "yet not what I will, but what you will' (v. 36). An angel appeared to strengthen him, lest the sorrow be too much for his human frame to bear (Luke 22:43).

The Betrayal and Arrest

14:42 Get up, let us go. Look! My betrayer is approaching!'

After his agonizing triumph in the garden of Gethsemane Jesus woke his disciples and went to meet his betrayer.

14:43 Right away, while Jesus was still speaking, Judas, one of the twelve, arrived. With him came a crowd armed with swords and clubs, sent by the chief priests and experts in the law and elders.

Even as he spoke, Judas arrived with a detachment of temple police, heavily armed. Judas may have had some idea of what the disciples' reactions to Jesus' arrest would be, particularly Peter's, and so he may have advised them to bring weapons.

14:44–46 (Now the betrayer had given them a sign, saying, 'The one I kiss is the man. Arrest him and lead him away under guard.') When Judas arrived, he went up to Jesus immediately and said, 'Rabbi!' and kissed him. Then they took hold of him and arrested him.

Judas had also agreed the means by which he would identify Jesus. The kiss was the usual form of greeting in New Testament times (Rom. 16:16); and among Christians such an affectionate greeting demonstrated love and brotherhood (1 Pet. 5:14). The callous way in which Judas used the kiss and hypocritically addressed Jesus as "Rabbi" demonstrated that he had gone beyond all hope of repentance (Prov. 27:6). In this way Judas handed the Saviour of the world into the hands of cruel men.

14:47 One of the bystanders drew his sword and struck the high priest's slave, cutting off his ear.

We are told in John 18:10 that it was Peter who made this useless attack upon Malchus, one of the high priest's servants, cutting off his ear. Luke informs us (Luke 22:51) that Jesus touched the ear of this servant and healed it immediately. Even to those who had come out to destroy him, Jesus showed love and compassion. The one who commands "love your enemies" (Matt. 5:44) never asks us to do anything which he did not do first.

14:48–49 Jesus said to them, 'Have you come with swords and clubs to arrest me like you would an outlaw? Day after day I was with you, teaching in the temple courts, yet you did not arrest me. But this has happened so that the scriptures would be fulfilled.'

Although it appeared that Judas was handing Jesus over to his enemies, and that his enemies now had Christ in their power, yet Jesus remained in complete control of the situation. He even dictated the terms of his own arrest, confounding his enemies by challenging them (John 18:7–8). Pointing to their weapons he reminds them that he was with them daily in the temple but they did not seize him. The fact that they had to come armed and under cover of darkness proved them to be in the wrong. Yet all things were happening in accordance with the scriptures: God was still in control.

14:50 Then all the disciples left him and fled.

Here we see the fulfilment of Jesus' prediction in verse 27; all the disciples left him and fled.

14:51–52 A young man was following him, wearing only a linen cloth. They tried to arrest him, but he ran off naked, leaving his linen cloth behind.

It is thought by some that this young man (who was probably in his teens) might have been Mark the writer of the gospel. The temple guards were unable to arrest him, but he only narrowly managed to escape by leaving his clothing behind.

The Religious Trial of Christ

After Jesus' arrest they took him first of all to Annas, who had retired as high priest fifteen years previously and was the father-in-law of the present high priest, Caiaphas (John 18:13). It was Caiaphas who had prophesied that it was needful that one man should die so that the whole nation should not perish (John 11:50–51). From there they led Jesus to Caiaphas, and the 71 members of the Sanhedrin (the religious authority of the Jews) assembled to put Jesus on trial, laying false charges against him.

14:54 And Peter had followed him from a distance, up to the high priest's courtyard. He was sitting with the guards and warming himself by the fire.

Peter, who originally had fled with the rest of the disciples in the garden, returned to follow Jesus at a safe distance and gained entry into the high priest's courtyard through John's influence (John 18:16). He sat among the enemies of Christ, warming himself by the fire.

14:55–56 The chief priests and the whole Sanhedrin were looking for evidence against Jesus so that they could put him to death, but they did not find anything. Many gave false testimony against him, but their testimony did not agree.

The very fact that they had difficulty finding any witnesses to give false testimony against Jesus proves that they could not justify his arrest. The text suggests that they were forced to bribe different people to make false accusations against Jesus; but even then these could not agree, God throwing their false testimony into confusion.

14:57–59 Some stood up and gave this false testimony against him: We heard him say, 'I will destroy this temple made with hands and in three days build another not made with hands.' Yet even on this point their testimony did not agree.

At last there were some who came forward to say that they had heard Jesus threaten to destroy the temple and then rebuild it. This was of course true, but in context, Jesus had been speaking of his death and resurrection. "Yet his death did destroy the need of the temple and established the church as a new place made without hands in which God would dwell" (Wesley Bible).

14:60–61 Then the high priest stood up before them and asked Jesus, 'Have you no answer? What is this that they are testifying against you?' But he was silent and did not answer. Again the high priest questioned him, 'Are you the Christ, the Son of the Blessed One?'

Caiaphas then took matters into his own hands, being amazed at Jesus' silent response to all the accusations being made against him (1 Pet. 2:23). If he had chosen to believe the scriptures, Caiaphas would have recognised Christ as the Son of God by his demeanour without having to question him (Isa. 53:7).

14:62 I am, said Jesus, and you will see the Son of Man sitting at the right hand of the Power and coming with the clouds of heaven.

Up until this point Jesus had not even let his own disciples openly confess him as Christ (Mark 8:30; Mark 9:9). But now there was no longer any need for concealment for his time had come. So Jesus answered with an emphatic "I am!" This claim to be the "I am", the deity, the messiah-King who was destined to sit at the right hand of God, from where he would come again in glory and judgement, was too much for the high priest.

14:63–64 Then the high priest tore his clothes and said, 'Why do we still need witnesses? You have heard the blasphemy! What is your verdict?' They all condemned him as deserving death.

Caiaphas could not have asked for any better. As far as he was concerned this was blasphemy, justification enough to condemn Jesus to death. And so it was by the religious leaders of his time that the Lord Jesus Christ was condemned to death.

14:65 Then some began to spit on him, and to blindfold him, and to strike him with their fists, saying, 'Prophesy!' The guards also took him and beat him.

The Sanhedrin had no power to carry out their sentence of death, for this could only be done by the Romans. Nevertheless, all restraint and respect for Jesus was abandoned as they abused him shamefully, spitting in his face (Isa. 50:6). They blindfolded him, asking him to prophecy who hit him. In this way he was despised, rejected and set at nought (Isa. 53:3).

Peter's Denial

14:66–67 Now while Peter was below in the courtyard, one of the high priest's slave girls came by. When she saw Peter warming himself, she looked directly at him and said, 'You also were with that Nazarene, Jesus.'

Whilst all this was going on, Peter was still warming himself by the fire, keeping company with those who were Christ's enemies. Nor did he go unnoticed, for a servant girl recognised him and accused him of being a follower of Jesus.

14:68 But he denied it: 'I don't even understand what you're talking about!' Then he went out to the gateway, and a rooster crowed.

Peter pretended that he didn't understand what she meant—this is the first denial—and the cock crew; Peter had begun to fall, just as Jesus had predicted.

14:69 When the slave girl saw him, she began again to say to the bystanders, 'This man is one of them.'

The girl was not going to let Peter get away with such a denial, and on seeing him again she made her accusation to others standing by that he was one of Jesus' followers.

14:70 But he denied it again. A short time later the bystanders again said to Peter, 'You must be one of them, because you are also a Galilean.'

This time, Peter denied that he was a disciple of Jesus—this was the second denial. The third time Peter was approached by those who stood with him, for his Galilean accent betrayed him. Surely, if he was a Galilean, he must be one of Christ's followers.

14:71–72 Then he began to curse, and he swore with an oath, 'I do not know this man you are talking about!' Immediately a rooster crowed a second time. Then Peter remembered what Jesus had said to him: 'Before a rooster crows twice, you will deny me three times.' And he broke down and wept.

On this third occasion Peter denied with oaths and curses that he ever knew Jesus at all—and the cock crowed again. Peter completely falls. At this point Luke reveals that Jesus looked at Peter—not with a look of condemnation but a look of love. It was enough; Peter remembered Jesus' prediction and was completely broken in spirit and wept. Like Jeremiah before him, Peter had learned to admit "my heart within me is broken" (Jer. 23:9). This was not to be the end of Peter; for his broken and contrite spirit and the fact that Jesus had prayed for him remained as his all-sufficient protection (Psalm 34:18).

Discussion Questions for Chapter 14

1. vv. 1–11. What effect did the love of Christ have on Mary?

Read each of the following sections again. What does each section tell you about the love of Jesus?

2. vv. 12–26.

3. vv. 27–31 & vv. 66–72

4. vv. 32–42.

5. vv. 43–65.

You will find suggested answers to the study questions on pages 183–193.

Mark Chapter 15

The Secular Trial of Christ

15:1 Early in the morning, after forming a plan, the chief priests with the elders and the experts in the law and the whole Sanhedrin tied Jesus up, led him away, and handed him over to Pilate.

The religious leaders had tried and condemned the Lord Jesus Christ to death but had no power to carry out the sentence. So they brought him before Pontius Pilate, the Roman governor of Judaea. If Pilate were to symbolize the rulers of the world (Ps. 2:2) then we might suggest that at Jesus' trial it was the world which was on trial before God. What would the world (symbolized by Pilate) choose to do with the only begotten Son of God? Notice that they tied Jesus up which shows that they still feared him.

15:2 So Pilate asked him, 'Are you the king of the Jews?' He replied, 'You say so.'

Luke tells us (Luke 23:2) that the false charges made against Jesus were that he was perverting the nation and forbidding the payment of taxes. However, the correct charges were that he claimed to be the Christ, a king. It is in response to the latter charges that Pilate questioned Jesus, for it was a crime for anyone to set themselves up as a king apart from Caesar. It is significant that Pilate did not ask Jesus if he claimed to be king of the Jews, but if he was king. Perhaps the majestic bearing of Christ had already introduced some uncertainty in Pilate's mind. At this point, Jesus freely acknowledged himself as king of the Jews. He is in fact the king of the whole earth (Jer. 23:5; Dan. 7:14); the "King of Kings" (Rev. 17:14).

15:3 Then the chief priests began to accuse him repeatedly.

There were many other accusations that the chief priests made against him, but Jesus did not answer them.

15:4–5 So Pilate asked him again, 'Have you nothing to say? See how many charges they are bringing against you!' But Jesus made no further reply, so that Pilate was amazed.

Christ's silence amazed Pilate, as it did Caiaphas in Mark 14:60; for he did not say another word. At this point, John informs us (John 18:38) that Pilate declared Jesus to be not guilty, for he could find no fault in him.

15:6–8 During the feast it was customary to release one prisoner to the people, whomever they requested. A man named Barabbas was imprisoned with rebels who had committed murder during an insurrection. Then the crowd came up and began to ask Pilate to release a prisoner for them, as was his custom.

More willing to please the people than to see justice done, Pilate puts the decision about Jesus' fate into the hands of a crowd which had already been made hostile by the chief priests. Wishing to avoid responsibility for Jesus' case, Pilate is conveniently reminded of the custom of releasing a prisoner at important festive occasions. Barabbas was a convicted criminal waiting to pay the death penalty for his crimes, just as all have sinned and come short of the glory of God (Rom. 3:23) and must pay the penalty of sin which is death (Rom. 6:23).

15:9–10 So Pilate asked them, 'Do you want me to release the king of the Jews for you?' (For he knew that the chief priests had handed him over because of envy.)

By using this custom Pilate made a weak effort to obtain the release of Jesus; for he knew that the chief priests had only accused him because they were jealous of him.

15:11–12 But the chief priests stirred up the crowd to have him release Barabbas instead. So Pilate spoke to them again, 'Then what do you want me to do with the one you call king of the Jews?'

Through the agitation of the priests, the crowd called out for the release of Barabbas. In reply, Pilate did what no good judge should ever do: he asked the crowd to decide Jesus' sentence. This is an example of mob rule at its worst.

15:13–14 They shouted back, 'Crucify him!' Pilate asked them, 'Why? What has he done wrong?' But they shouted more insistently, 'Crucify him!'

"Crucify him!" they cried. "Why?" Pilate asked, "What has he done wrong?" But to the crowd, it didn't matter what he had done. He may have done no wrong, but "crucify him anyway!" is effectively the crowd's reply.

Through all these events, Jesus knew that he was neither at the mercy of Pilate, nor of the crowds, for he was in the hands of God, and all that was happening was his Father's will in fulfilment of Scripture: "it pleased the Lord to bruise him" (Isa. 53:10).

15:15 Because he wanted to satisfy the crowd, Pilate released Barabbas for them. Then, after he had Jesus flogged, he handed him over to be crucified.

Like Barabbas, sinners today can be released and escape death through the crucifixion of the Lord Jesus who has paid sin's penalty for all sinners (Gal. 3:13). Before the crucifixion, Pilate ordered that Jesus be flogged; that is, beaten with a whip made of leather thongs which is said to have had pieces of bone or metal on the ends. This was often given to people who had committed serious crimes and sometimes led to their death before being crucified. Peter refers to this the scourging as in some way being the source of our healing (Isa. 50:6; 53:5; 1 Pet. 2:24).

15:16–19 So the soldiers led him into the palace (that is, the governor's residence) and called together the whole cohort. They put a purple cloak on him and after braiding a crown of thorns, they put it on him. They began to salute him: 'Hail, king of the Jews!' Again and again they struck him on the head with a staff and spit on him. Then they knelt down and paid homage to him.

Jesus was next handed over to the Roman soldiers for them to do with as they wanted. Taking him into the Praetorium, a judgement hall attached to Pilate's house, they called the whole garrison together to mock him, as he had predicted (Mark 10:34). Purple was the royal colour, so they gave Jesus a purple robe. Kings wore crowns, so they made him a crown of thorns and gave him a reed as a sceptre of authority (Matt. 27:29). They paid mocking homage to him and bowed their knees to him. Not one of these soldiers could have known that Jesus was the beloved Son of God and that all power and authority was his, and that he would come again in glory as their almighty judge (2 Tim. 4:1).

15:20 When they had finished mocking him, they stripped him of the purple cloak and put his own clothes back on him. Then they led him away to crucify him.

When they had finished they took it all from him and led him out to be crucified.

The Lamb of God Sacrificed for the Sins of the World

15:21 The soldiers forced a passer-by to carry his cross, Simon of Cyrene, who was coming in from the country (he was the father of Alexander and Rufus).

Simon would have been a Jew from the city of Cyrene (in North Africa) visiting Jerusalem for the Passover with his sons, Alexander and Rufus. A Rufus is mentioned by Paul in Romans 16:13, though it is not certainly the same one.

15:22 They brought Jesus to a place called Golgotha (which is translated, 'Place of the Skull').

Simon was compelled by the Romans to carry the cross of Christ to a place called in Aramaic "Golgotha", or in Latin "Calvary", both names meaning "the place of the skull".

15:23 They offered him wine mixed with myrrh, but he did not take it.

Before nailing him to the cross they offered him a mixture of wine and myrrh (myrrh would have dulled the pain) but he refused it for he had to experience complete suffering (Ps. 69:21).

15:24 Then they crucified him and divided his clothes, throwing dice for them, to decide what each would take.

When they had nailed him to the cross, having stripped him of his clothing, they cast lots (using a type of dice) to determine who should get what (Ps. 22:18).

15:25 It was nine o'clock in the morning when they crucified him.

At nine o'clock in the morning they lifted him up and the crucifixion began (John 3:14).

15:26 The inscription of the charge against him read, 'The king of the Jews.'

It was the practice of the Romans to write the crime which had been committed above the head of the criminal; thus it was with Jesus. Although the priests objected to this, Pilate insisted that it should remain (John 19:21).

15:27–28 With Him they also crucified two robbers, one on His right and the other on His left. So the Scripture was fulfilled which says, "And He was numbered with the transgressors." (NKJV™)

In fulfilment of the scripture, on either side of him two robbers were crucified (Isaiah 53:12).

15:29–30 Those who passed by defamed him, shaking their heads and saying, 'Aha! You, who can destroy the temple and rebuild it in three days, save yourself and come down from the cross!'

How evil the hearts of wicked men must be; for they did not cease to mock Christ even as he hung on the cross. They mocked him, saying that although he had claimed that he would destroy and rebuild the temple in three days, he was unable to help himself.

15:31–32 In the same way even the chief priests — together with the experts in the law — were mocking him among themselves: 'He saved others, but he cannot save himself! Let the Christ, the king of Israel, come down from the cross now, that we may see and believe!' Those who were crucified with him also spoke abusively to him.

The chief priests joined in the ridicule, tempting Christ to save himself from death, just as he had saved others. The claim that they would believe what they saw is in fact a contradiction, for faith does not involve seeing (Heb. 11:1). The reality was that if Christ had wanted to, he could have come down from the cross by calling more than 12 legions of angels to come to his aid (Matt. 26:53).

15:33 Now when it was noon, darkness came over the whole land until three in the afternoon.

From noon to three o'clock in the afternoon darkness covered the whole land as the Son of Man became sin for us and bore the penalty of sin on the cross.

15:34 Around three o'clock Jesus cried out with a loud voice, 'Eloi, Eloi, lama sabachthani?' which means, 'My God, my God, why have you forsaken me?'

At three o'clock in the afternoon Jesus cried "My God, my God, why have you forsaken me?" (Ps. 22:1); for at this point he experienced the wrath of God against all sin on behalf of sinners. Some commentators say that Jesus suffered all the pangs of hell during the three hours of darkness. Those who reject Jesus Christ as their Saviour will experience being forsaken by God when they are in hell.

15:35–36 When some of the bystanders heard it they said, 'Listen, he is calling for Elijah!' Then someone ran, filled a sponge with sour wine, put it on a stick, and gave it to him to drink, saying, 'Leave him alone! Let's see if Elijah will come to take him down!'

Some bystanders mistook Jesus' cry as a call for help from Elijah and waited to see if Elijah would set him free. In response to his cry "I thirst" (John 19:28) they gave him sour wine (Ps. 69:21).

15:37 But Jesus cried out with a loud voice and breathed his last.

This drink enabled Jesus to make his final cry from the cross. Only John records the words of that cry: "it is finished" (John 19:30). Christ had completed the work of salvation according to his Father's plan; giving up his life so that sinners might be redeemed. Ultimately it was neither the religious leaders, nor the people crying "crucify him", nor Pilate nor the Roman soldiers that took his life—for he gave it (John 10:18).

15:38 And the temple curtain was torn in two, from top to bottom.

The moment Jesus died the veil that barred the way into the Holy of Holies, the presence of God, was torn in two as God accepted the once and for all sacrifice of his Son for the sins of the world (Heb. 10:10).

15:39 Now when the centurion, who stood in front of him, saw how he died, he said, 'Truly this man was God's Son!'

It was the centurion, a Gentile, who after the crucifixion was the first to acknowledge that Jesus was the Son of God.

15:40–41 There were also women, watching from a distance. Among them were Mary Magdalene, and Mary the mother of James the younger and of Joses, and Salome. When he was in Galilee, they had followed him and given him support. Many other women who had come up with him to Jerusalem were there too.

Mark closes this section by telling us the names of the women who had followed Jesus and who were with him at the end; being eye-witnesses of his sufferings. Among them was Mary, his mother, to whom Simeon prophesied (when she presented Jesus in the temple) that her heart would be pierced through with a sword of grief as she beheld him being crucified (Luke 2:35).

Christ's Burial

Having become sin for us, Jesus took sin to the cross where it was put to death and then buried (Rom. 6:3–8). This burial was also according to the scriptures (Isa. 53:9), and served as proof that he had indeed died.

15:42 Now when evening had already come, since it was the day of preparation (that is, the day before the Sabbath),

The Jewish day was from sunset to sunset. Jesus died at about three o'clock in the afternoon on the preparation day for the Sabbath. To leave a body hanging on the cross over the Sabbath would be a desecration of the day; which is why the Jews asked Pilate to break the legs of those who were crucified to make certain they were dead so that they could be buried before sunset. When they came to Jesus they found him already dead so there was no need to break his bones (John 19:31–36; Ps. 34:20).

15:43 Joseph of Arimathea, a highly regarded member of the council, who was himself looking forward to the kingdom of God, went boldly to Pilate and asked for the body of Jesus.

Joseph of Arimathea, a wealthy member of the Sanhedrin, who until now had been a secret follower of Jesus, came right out in the open, and went boldly to Pilate to ask for the body of Jesus.

15:44–45 Pilate was surprised that he was already dead. He called the centurion and asked him if he had been dead for some time. When Pilate was informed by the centurion, he gave the body to Joseph.

Pilate could not believe that Jesus had died already; it usually took a few days for someone to die by crucifixion. So he sent for the centurion in charge, who confirmed that Jesus was dead.

15:46 After Joseph bought a linen cloth and took down the body, he wrapped it in the linen and placed it in a tomb cut out of the rock. Then he rolled a stone across the entrance of the tomb.

Then Joseph and Nicodemus (another secret follower) took the body of Jesus down from the cross and embalmed it according to Jewish burial customs (John 19:39–40). They placed it in a tomb which Joseph had originally prepared for himself. A huge stone was rolled across the opening and, at the request of the chief priests, was sealed. A guard was also set over the tomb, since the Jewish leaders feared that Jesus would rise from the dead as he had said (Matt. 27:62–65).

15:47 Mary Magdalene and Mary the mother of Joses saw where the body was placed.

Two of the women watched all this so that they knew where to come back after the Sabbath to anoint the body.

Discussion Questions for Chapter 15

1. vv. 1–5. Why do you think Jesus remained silent during his trials before the chief priests and before Pilate? What effect did his silence have on them?

2. vv. 16–25. Consider Jesus' sufferings. In what way might it be said that Jesus was in control through all of his sufferings?

3. vv. 33–37. What do you think was significant about Jesus' cry, "My God, my God, why have you forsaken me?"

4. v. 38. What was significant about the tearing in two of the temple curtain?

5. vv.42–47. What impresses you most as you read the details about Jesus' burial?

You will find suggested answers to the study questions on pages 183–193.

Mark Chapter 16

The Resurrection

16:1–3 When the Sabbath was over, Mary Magdalene, Mary the mother of James, and Salome bought aromatic spices so that they might go and anoint him. And very early on the first day of the week, at sunrise, they went to the tomb. They had been asking each other, 'Who will roll away the stone for us from the entrance to the tomb?'

Having rested on the Sabbath in obedience to God's command, the women came to Jesus' tomb on the third day (Sunday) as the sun began to rise. They had stood faithfully at Jesus' cross and were present at his burial; and now they had returned to anoint his body with spices. They had been wondering who would roll away the stone for them; which indicates that they certainly did not expect his resurrection. They may have been aware, however, that guards were watching the tomb.

16:4–5 But when they looked up, they saw that the stone, which was very large, had been rolled back. Then as they went into the tomb, they saw a young man dressed in a white robe sitting on the right side; and they were alarmed.

On arriving at the tomb, they found that the stone had already been rolled away. Matthew indicates (Matt. 28:2) that there was a great earthquake, and that an angel descended to roll away the stone, paralysing the guards with fear. On entering the tomb, they found the angel still there and they too became afraid.

16:6–7 But he said to them, 'Do not be alarmed. You are looking for Jesus the Nazarene, who was crucified. He has been raised! He is not here. Look, there is the place where they laid him. But go; tell his disciples, even Peter, that he is going ahead of you into Galilee. You will see him there, just as he told you.'

It was the angel who first announced that Jesus was raised from the dead and instructed the women to bring this news to his disciples. Even though they had all forsaken him, and Peter in particular had denied him, Jesus would go ahead of them into Galilee just as he promised that he would (Mark 14:28). "Jesus is always ready to restore those who forsake him if they turn to him in faith to make a new start" (Wesley Bible).

16:8 Then they went out and ran from the tomb, for terror and bewilderment had seized them. And they said nothing to anyone, because they were afraid.

The women ran from the empty tomb filled with an awesome fear for they realised that God had been at work in a mighty way. They did not do as the angel had bidden them straight away because of this fear.

The resurrection of Christ is of immense importance to the believer. By it Jesus was declared to be the Son of God with power (Rom. 1:4). Because Christ lives we live also with eternal, abundant life. We are justified before God since Christ's resurrection shows that he has accepted the death of his Son as the penalty paid for our sin (Rom. 4:25). We cannot be saved unless we believe in the resurrection (Rom. 10:9). We have a sure hope that we too shall be raised (2 Cor. 4:14; 1 Pet. 1:3).

His Appearances

16:9 Early on the first day of the week, after he arose, he appeared first to Mary Magdalene, from whom he had driven out seven demons.

The first person Jesus showed himself to after his resurrection was Mary Magdalene, from whom he had cast seven demons. Either she had stayed behind after the other women had gone or she had later returned to the garden.

16:10–11 She went out and told those who were with him, while they were mourning and weeping. And when they heard that he was alive and had been seen by her, they did not believe.

It was Mary who went to tell the disciples, who were even then mourning his death, that he was risen. Yet they did not believe her, in spite of the fact that Jesus had told them a number of times that he would rise from the dead after three days.

16:12–13 After this he appeared in a different form to two of them while they were on their way to the country. They went back and told the rest, but they did not believe them.

Jesus next appeared to two disciples on the road to Emmaus as they returned home. They failed to recognise him until he had broken bread with them (Luke 24:13–31). They went to tell the others that they had seen the Lord but these disciples were still full of unbelief.

16:14 Then he appeared to the eleven themselves, while they were eating, and he rebuked them for their unbelief and hardness of heart, because they did not believe those who had seen him resurrected.

Finally, Jesus appeared to the eleven disciples at a meal and rebuked them for their lack of faith and hardness of heart (Heb. 3:12).

The Great Commission

16:15 He said to them, 'Go into all the world and preach the gospel to every creature.

Although these disciples had deserted him, were unbelieving, hard hearted and weak, it was to them that Jesus committed the preaching of the gospel to the whole world. What changed them into fearless believing witnesses was their experience of being filled with the Holy Spirit (Acts 1:8).

16:16 The one who believes and is baptized will be saved, but the one who does not believe will be condemned.

All who believe the gospel message will be saved. They must be baptised in water and will receive the gift of the Holy Spirit (Acts 2:38).

Those who do not believe will be judged (John 12:48) and cast into the lake of fire (Rev. 20:15).

16:17–18 These signs will accompany those who believe: In my name they will drive out demons; they will speak in new languages; they will pick up snakes with their hands, and whatever poison they drink will not harm them; they will place their hands on the sick and they will be well.'

Jesus' promise was given to all who believe in his name. They will perform many signs and wonders; being empowered to cast out demons, and to speak with new tongues. They will be able to handle serpents and not be harmed (Acts 28:3–6). Being poisoned shall not affect them; and they will lay hands on the sick and they will get well.

The Ascension

16:19 After the Lord Jesus had spoken to them, he was taken up into heaven and sat down at the right hand of God.

Jesus appeared to his disciples for forty days following his resurrection, giving them further teaching and instructions. On the fortieth day he led them to Mount Olivet, from whence he was received up into heaven (Acts 1:9–12) and sat at the right hand of God. God has highly exalted his Son and given a name that is above every other name (Phil. 2:9). In heaven, Jesus ever lives to make intercession for his people (Heb. 7:25) and one day he will come again to take us to our heavenly home, where we will forever be with our Lord and Saviour (1 Thess. 4:16–17).

16:20 They went out and proclaimed everywhere, while the Lord worked with them and confirmed the word through the accompanying signs.

When we read the book of Acts we see further details of Mark's claim here. The disciples obeyed the command to go and preach; and as they did, Jesus worked with them and confirmed his gospel in miraculous ways. This will always be the case when Christians take Christ's command seriously and go into the entire world to preach the gospel.

Discussion Questions for Chapter 16

1. v1. Why do you think the women wanted to anoint Jesus' body?

2. vv. 1–8. The women never did get to anoint the body of Jesus. Describe the events of that resurrection Sunday as recorded by Mark.

3. vv. 9–14. Why do you think the disciples failed to believe the reports that Jesus was alive from the dead?

4. vv. 15–20. What great task has Jesus entrusted to his disciples until he comes again?

5. Why do you think Mark wrote his gospel?

You will find suggested answers to the study questions on pages 183–193.

Suggested Answers to Discussion Questions

Chapter 1

1. In this section of Mark's gospel, Mark himself, John the Baptist, God himself and even a demon give witness in various ways that Jesus Christ is the Son of God.

2. We do not know much about Jesus' earthly life until this point—but concerning all that Jesus had done during his lifetime God's verdict was that he was well pleased. Since God is never pleased with sin, we can be sure that Jesus Christ was without sin.

3. Mark shows Jesus to be someone greater than John firstly by his introduction—only Jesus is referred to as the son of God; and the gospel is all about him. Mark depicts John as a messenger or herald. In those days a herald was sent before a king to announce his coming; here John is the servant and Jesus is the king. John himself declares Jesus to be mightier and more worthy than he was. John has no miraculous sign to confirm his identity, whereas the Spirit descends and God speaks from heaven to confirm Jesus' identity. Mark also shows Jesus' power over sickness and unclean spirits—something which had never been seen before, not even in John's ministry.

4. I think Jesus understood that his calling was to reach the whole of Israel and not just Capernaum. Also, whilst he delighted to heal people (for the good of their bodies) he realised that it was more important to teach the people for the good of their souls.

5. In the first chapter of Mark, Christ demonstrates his authority through his teaching about God, and by his power over evil spirits and sickness.

Chapter 2

1. The forgiveness of sins brings a person near to God eternally, and so is far more important than the healing of a body which will only last a lifetime. Jesus knew which was more important to this man.

2. The Pharisees thought themselves holy and so complained when Jesus ate with tax collectors and sinners—they would never do such a thing! They wrongly thought that contact with sinners would make them unclean—whereas in reality it was the pride and sinfulness of their own hearts which made them unclean. What is especially bad is that these Pharisees claimed to teach the people about God—but in their self-righteousness they had no time to instruct those who had gone astray and bring them back to God, as Jesus did.

3. According to Jesus, it was the wrong time for his disciples to fast since he was still with them. They would begin to fast when he had returned to heaven.

4. I think that Jesus is teaching that no amount of religious good works can fix our broken relationship with God. Jesus can provide us with a new nature which can "contain" a new relationship with God.

5. Personally, I tend to keep Sunday as a Sabbath day and do no work but the work of ministry. For example, we do no housework on this day, and my wife does not go to work in her shop. More importantly, we use the time to go to church for worship, fellowship and Bible study.

Chapter 3

1. The Pharisees had hardened their hearts and refused to accept Christ even in the face of overwhelming evidence. They had become blinded by their own ideas of what it meant to be righteous or religious.

2. Although he was God's son Jesus submitted himself to God's guidance that he might do God's will. It was necessary for Jesus to pray before

appointing the twelve since he knew that their appointment must be made by God's sanction.

3. We are not sure why Jesus' family thought that he was mad. Perhaps it was because of the way he had left everything to travel and teach about God, or because of the miracles he did and the large crowds which he attracted. Perhaps they thought the strain would be too much for him.

4. Satan can only be cast out by someone who is stronger than he is—and this can only be God. It is by the power of the Holy Spirit that demons are cast out, and they leave by compunction.

5. Someone who is part of God's family will want to be with Jesus, hear his word and do God's will. Since they are part of one family, their main characteristic is love.

Chapter 4

1. The seed is the word of God, or the gospel of Jesus Christ. When it is honestly received this seed produces the fruits of faith and obedience to God.

2. When there is a lamp on in the room, the whole room receives the light. When someone has genuinely received Christ, there will be "fruit" or evidence of this reality shown in their lives. In terms of our witnessing for Christ, the parable shows that it is our changed lives as much as our words which can influence others for Jesus.

3. The power of God for salvation is contained within the gospel of Christ, like a seed which has life in itself. It is God, not the farmer who makes the seed grow, and so it is God, not the preacher, who works continually (day and night) to produce fruit from his word and bring people to salvation.

4. The mustard seed is very small, but the word of the gospel is not visible at all. Yet just as the small seed grows to produce a tree, so the invisible seed

provides visible evidence of its life giving properties by the transformed lives of those who receive it.

Chapter 5

1. What impresses me most about how Jesus delivered the man of Gadara is that he only needed a simple, quiet word to do this. Also, it seems Jesus travelled a long way through a storm specifically to reach this man who had been ostracised by others.

2. I think the people of Gadara asked Jesus to leave their region because they were terrified of what they could not understand—his supernatural power.

3. Through the witness of this one man, the fear the people of Decapolis had of Jesus was transformed into openness and a desire to receive his blessing.

4. Jairus' position as ruler of the synagogue made it difficult for him to come to Jesus. It may well have cost him his livelihood and respect. But he finally came as his care for his daughter outweighed any care he had for his own dignity or situation.

5. The woman with the issue of blood teaches us to have tenacious faith and be persistent in seeking what we want from God. She did not stop to ask, but took her healing from Jesus.

Chapter 6

1. Jesus sent his apostles to preach that people should repent, and to cast out devils and heal the sick.

2. Remaining a faithful witness to Jesus Christ cost John his freedom and ultimately his life.

3. I think the apostles may have been elated with their own success when they returned to Jesus.

4. The feeding of the 5,000 teaches us to make ourselves available to serve Christ; giving him whatever we have, no matter how little it seems, so that he can break, bless and use us in his own miraculous way to make us witnesses for his glory.

5. vv. 45–52. Jesus walking on the water proved him to be more than a mere man; it demonstrated his supernatural power as Lord of Creation.

vv. 53–56. The healing of the multitudes in Gennesaret shows the success in that region of the witness of the man whom Jesus had earlier delivered from demons. It also shows Christ's compassion and the inexhaustibility of his power – all who came in faith were healed.

Chapter 7

1. Since sin finds its origin in the heart and not the body, outward religious rituals such as washing can never take away our sins.

2. The fact that Jesus died on the cross shedding his blood is the way God has provided for our sins to be cleansed.

3. Some of the religious instruction given by the Pharisees ran contrary to the commandments of God, especially concerning the financial support of parents.

4. Whatever enters a person's body goes into the stomach to be digested, and the waste passes from the body. This is a physical process, but humans are spiritual beings. It is the sinful attitude of our heart, and the resulting in outward actions, which make us unclean in God's sight.

5. The Syrophoenician woman humbly acknowledged that she had no rightful claims on Jesus; yet she had faith that he would freely grant her request. Her request was very specific concerning her daughter; and she persisted, refusing to take no for an answer, until Jesus met her need.

Chapter 8

1. I think that Jesus repeated his earlier miracle because the people were slow to believe. He may also have wanted to show by this repetition that he was willing to give to all people, and not only a chosen few.

2. The Pharisees demanded signs from Jesus because they stubbornly refused to believe in him despite overwhelming evidence of his divine credentials.

3. False teaching is like yeast because a very little soon spreads throughout the church. As yeast causes dough to swell, so false teaching leads to the swelling of rebellion and disobedience against God.

4. I honestly don't know! I wonder whether the blind man's lack of faith led to his healing occurring in two stages; on the other hand, perhaps there were two causes of his condition which Jesus chose to heal separately.

5. To truly follow Jesus Christ we must be prepared to die to self-will, letting go of our own desires and ambitions, allowing them to be replaced by God's desires and plans for our lives. Such a way of life will usually lead to opposition or even persecution from others.

Chapter 9

1. When they failed to deliver a boy who was possessed with an evil spirit, the disciples learned that the power to cast out demons was not in themselves, but in Christ; and that they could only use that power inasmuch as they had faith in Christ. Difficult cases like this could only be successfully dealt with by prayer, fasting and total dependence on God.

2. According to Jesus, the greatest in the kingdom of God would be the one who saw themselves as the least, and who did most to serve their fellow believers.

3. John wanted to stop a man doing miracles in Jesus name because he was not "one of the club". John failed to realise that Jesus' power would one day become available to all believers by faith.

4. Jesus told John that whoever was preaching or doing miracles in his name was working on the same side as them, and so should not be hindered. Even if such a person were not recognised as part of the church, their work would be of benefit to the church.

5. Jesus wanted his followers to have a zero tolerance attitude toward sin, rooting it out of the experience of their lives.

Chapter 10

1. According to Jesus, marriage originated with God who "made them male and female" and was meant to last a lifetime.

2. Since Jesus saw marriage as being ordained of God for lifetime, he permitted separation only on the grounds of infidelity—and even then he did not seem to approve of re-marriage

3. Yes, children are able to enter the kingdom of God in the same way as adults—by faith in Jesus Christ.

4. The young man was sad when Jesus told him that to give all his money to the poor because he loved his money more than he wanted eternal life, and he knew he could not part with it.

5. Jesus promises that all those who leave everything to follow him will be rewarded in this present life by the blessings they receive and share with the church; and also with eternal life in the age to come.

Chapter 11

1. As Jesus entered Jerusalem he rode on a young donkey which no one had ever previously ridden. The disciples cut down palm leaves and placed these

together with their coats on the road like a pathway before him, and shouted praise to God with loud voices, saying "Hosanna!"

2. God expect to find the fruit of repentance, obedience and faith in response to Jesus' message among those who lived in Jerusalem. Instead, Jesus found only unbelief, hardness of heart and rejection.

3. Jesus was angry because the temple was to be a holy place of worship and prayer. To profane God's place of worship was, for Jesus, to insult God and profane his name.

4. The disciples' prayers would be successful as they had faith that they would receive the answer to their prayers. However, unforgiveness and unbelief would hinder their prayers.

5. The Pharisees opposed Jesus' authority because it undermined their own.

Chapter 12

1. God had made Israel his own people and given them the land to live in. He gave them his word and many godly leaders to teach them his ways. He sent many prophets who taught the people to repent and return to give God his due in terms of obedience and worship—but they would not. Instead they abused and killed the prophets. When God finally sent his own Son to them, they refused to listen and obey him too, casting him out and crucifying him. For this, God would punish them.

2. Taxes are used to support government and the works of the state. Christians are to play an active part in the society in which they live, even though they are citizens of heaven.

3. The greatest commandment is to love God with all your heart, soul and mind, and your neighbour as yourself.

4. The Christ is greater than David or all the prophets, for he is the Son of God.

5. The widow's offering was worth more to God than all the others because of the way in which it was given—with genuine love as an act of worship; in faith, since she then had to depend on God to meet her needs; and with humility and sincerity, for she did not give in order for others to see.

Chapter 13

1. Any one on earth claiming to be Christ is false, since Jesus is at this time in heaven; and it is from there, coming on the clouds of heaven in power and glory, visible to everyone, that he will return.

2. Jesus said that false Christs, wars, famines, earthquakes and the persecution of the church would be the signs that his coming was drawing near.

3. These will be days of great trouble, and Jesus' description of them centre on Jerusalem and Judea, where the Jews will need to flee from a false Christ who will seize power and seek to destroy them. Never before and never again will anyone experience such a time of suffering.

4. People can recognise the natural signs that summer is coming, or that the seasons are changing; in a similar way Jesus wants people to be alert to the signs that his coming is drawing near.

5. No one can correctly predict the time of Jesus' coming, for it is known only to God the Father and will not be revealed to humanity.

Chapter 14

1. The love of Christ provoked gratitude and reciprocal love from Mary; and Mary was inwardly compelled to express these feelings in actions which demonstrated her love for Jesus.

2. Jesus' love for his disciples was fervent and personal.

3. Jesus' love was given in spite of the failings of his disciples and his concern for them was constant—in spite of what he suffered he still thought of his own.

4. Jesus' love for his Father was so great that he was prepared to obey even to the point of death by crucifixion, and his love for us was so great that he was prepared to offer himself for us on the cross.

5. Jesus' love made him face arrest and shame alone for our sakes.

Chapter 15

1. I think Jesus remained silent during his trial before the chief priests because he had nothing further to say to them. He was in God's hands not theirs, doing his Father's will. Answering their false charges might have made it seem that they were in control, whereas Jesus knew that God was. His silence amazed them.

2. I think Jesus was in control even during his sufferings because he had foretold all that was going to happen to him. He continued to love his enemies throughout all of his sufferings.

3. When Jesus cried, "My God, my God, why have you forsaken me?" he was revealing the depth of his suffering, being made sin for all humanity, tasting death on our behalf.

4. The temple curtain was torn open to reveal that through Jesus' death the way to God had been forever opened.

5. Jesus was given the burial of a ruler, not of a criminal, by a council member who seemed no longer afraid to show his deep regard for Jesus.

Chapter 16

1. The women wanted to anoint Jesus body to show their love for him and express their grief.

2. When the women came to the garden, to anoint the body of Jesus, an angel came and rolled away the stone from the tomb, and announced to them that Jesus was no longer dead but alive.

3. The disciples had failed to believe Jesus own words concerning his resurrection, even though they had seen Jesus raise others from the dead— so they were unlikely to believe the women. The gospels say that later Jesus rebuked their hardness of heart. Perhaps their grief and shock at the way in which he died may have contributed to this hardening.

4. Jesus has entrusted all believers with the task of preaching the gospel to every person until he comes again.

5. I think Mark wrote his gospel so that those who read it might believe in the Lord Jesus Christ and have eternal life.

Bibliography

1. Albert Barnes *Notes on the Bible* (Taken from e-Sword. Rick Meyers, 2000)

2. Robert Jamieson, A.R. Fausset and David Brown *Commentary Critical and Explanatory on the Whole Bible* (Taken from e-Sword. Rick Meyers, 2000)

3. Matthew Henry *Concise Commentary on the Whole Bible* (Taken from e-Sword. Rick Meyers, 2000)

4. A.T. Robertson *Word Pictures in the New Testament* (Taken from e-Sword. Rick Meyers, 2000)

5. M.R. Vincent D.D. *Vincent's Word Studies* (Taken from e-Sword. Rick Meyers, 2000)

6. W.E. Vine *Expository Dictionary of New Testament Words* (Oliphants, 1940)

7. John Wesley *Explanatory Notes on the Whole Bible* (Taken from e-Sword. Rick Meyers, 2000)

8. Amplified New Testament (Amp. N. T.) (Zondervan, 1987)

9. The Living Bible (Taken from e-Sword. Rick Meyers, 2000)

10. The King James Version of the Bible (KJV) (Taken from e-Sword. Rick Meyers, 2000)

11. A Cole. Mark

Appendix – How to Use this Study Guide

Good Bible study takes time. Set aside a sufficient time to study the chapter on your own – or divide the chapter into two parts. Allow an hour if possible or at least half an hour for your study.

We recommend that you photocopy the discussion questions (or print them from www.biblestudiesonline.org.uk). Use one for yourself, and distribute one each to every member of your study group. Having studied the verses on your own, arrange a meeting so you can join together and compare notes.

Always pray before you begin your study, that God will give you understanding. Then read the chapter itself, from whichever Bible version you prefer. Then sit down, in a quiet place, and read through each verse again together with the guide notes, taking time to reflect and think upon what you read. Make your own notes if possible; recording what God is showing you through the chapter, which might be somewhat different to the guide notes, especially if something is speaking to you personally from a certain verse or chapter. Be sure to share these insights later with your Bible study group. Again, close your study time with a short prayer. Remember that God himself is your greatest teacher, so you need to spend time with him if you wish to understand his word.

We recommend that you concentrate on no more than one chapter at a time. Reading the verses through again will help to ensure that what you have learned will stay in your heart and become part of your life.

Remember—God's word is not an academic textbook to be learned by rote. It is a living word to be hidden in your heart and obeyed in your life. May God bless you as you seek to follow him, employing the best method for spiritual growth which has ever been known to humankind—Bible study!

BV - #0024 - 240326 - C0 - 216/138/11 - PB - 9781910942086 - Gloss Lamination